TODAY'S CHURCH

Stanley Woodhead

ARTHUR H. STOCKWELL LTD.
Elms Court   Ilfracombe   Devon
Established 1898

Unless otherwise stated, Scripture quotations
are from the King James version of the Bible.

ISBN 0 7223 2711-0

Printed in Great Britain by
Arthur H. Stockwell Ltd.
Elms Court   Ilfracombe
Devon

THANKS

My thanks are due to several friends who have commented on the original manuscript:

To Eric Hallsworth, who typed Part 1.

To Albert Balding, who typed Parts 2 and 3, corrected the proofs and handled the approach to potential publishers.

Also to my lifelong friend Derwent Sharpe, who was the first person to introduce me to the idea that the Bible is true.

Without confidence in the truth of the Bible, this little work would certainly not have come into being.

A PRAYER

"It is time for Thee, Lord, to work: for they have made void Thy law. Therefore I love Thy commandments above gold; yea, above fine gold. Therefore I esteem all Thy precepts concerning all things to be right; and I hate every false way".

So wrote The Psalmist in Ps. 119:126—128.

FOREWORD:— STANLEY WOODHEAD

One of the things I noticed first about Stanley Woodhead when I met him at work, was that sense of controlled power that can be seen at a hydro-electric scheme. There seems to be an enormous reserve, but one can only see a trickle of water flowing down that gigantic dam; so it was with Stanley. After my conversion, I came to understand the phenomenon; this meek, quiet man was energised by the Holy Spirit.

When the Workers Christian Fellowship was formed, he was undoubtedly the shepherd with all these young lambs, yet he appeared to be almost naive in a simple, straightforward belief in all the Bible. I have no doubt that the many and varied problems that arose among the Christians, most of them fairly well educated, would never have been resolved with so much sympathy and encouragement without that belief and his complete trust in the Christ he loves.

This little book embodies such confidence, coupled with a desire that the true New-Testament Church should emerge Holy Spirit guided, controlled and empowered to declare, in what may well be the last days that the Body of Jesus on earth is very much alive and healthy.

I will always treasure the friendship — yes brotherhood — I enjoy with Stanley, who has helped me to look over the shoulders of all the traditions and ceremonies of men to see the honest and appealing face of the Saviour they sometimes seem to hide.

You may not like all you read; as he says, "You're in for some shocks", but if these bring you nearer to the "perfect" church and drive you to the scriptures to see "if these things be so", then you too will gain a little of my appreciation of this meek and mighty man — and perhaps also learn, with the "trees of the field", to clap your hands to the Glory of God.

Albert Balding.

List of Illustrations

CONTENTS

PART 1   *TODAY'S CHURCH -- GOD'S DESIGN*

PART 2   *THE AUTHOR'S EXPERIENCES*

Part 1

TODAY'S CHURCH - - GOD'S DESIGN

Chapter 1 — INTRODUCTION

Yes, certainly the Church is God's invention. Moreover it is His creation and we are told that 'the gates of hell shall not prevail' against it — which is comforting, especially in view of the magnitude of the opposition it has met and is meeting.

This little book aims at giving comfort, courage and strength as the reader is brought face to face with the word of God concerning the Church of God. But be warned and prepared for some surprises, if not downright shocks!

In Isaiah 55:8 & 9 we read, "For my thoughts are not your thoughts, neither are your ways my ways, saith the Lord. For as the heavens are higher than the earth, so are my ways higher than your ways, and my thoughts than your thoughts." And in 1 Cor. 1:25 we read, "the foolishness of God is wiser than men; and the weakness of God is stronger than men."

There are many instances in scripture where God's strategy would appear foolish. For example, what would be more foolish than to attempt to bring down the walls of besieged Jericho by marching round them thirteen times blowing trumpets and shouting? But God had a man willing to obey Him, and down came the walls! Or what would be more foolish than to attempt to cross the Red Sea without boats or aeroplanes? But God had a man willing to obey Him — and the children of Israel got across — without getting wet! (The first of these incidents is recorded in Josh. 6:1—16, and the second in Ex. 14:15—28). In each of these instances, God found a man who would obey Him, a man who would face scorn and ridicule and persecution.

11

Chapter 2 — THE CHURCH, THE WAY GOD DESIGNED IT

By the "the Church" we refer to the complete body of all believers in Christ Jesus who are twice-born, regardless of denomination, and who have Christ and the Holy Spirit dwelling in them. It is not a natural company, but a supernatural company, because God forms part of it by dwelling in it. If it were a natural company we could devise a system of government that would be appropriate. All that would be needed would be clever, eloquent, well-educated men to rule over appropriate-sized groups, such as we have in the armed forces.

But it is not a natural company, and it needs the wisdom of God to organise it.

The Church is a very costly thing, a very precious thing to God. It cost Him the sacrifice of His Son, His only begotten Son. It is destined to be the Bride of Christ — Revn. 19:7. It wears special invisible robes for it is clothed with humility — 1 Pet. 5:5. It makes invisible sacrifices to God: the sacrifice of praise — Heb. 13:15. It grows invisible fruit:— love, joy, peace, long-suffering, gentleness, goodness, faith, meekness, temperance — Gal. 5:22, 23. All its members teach and admonish one another (or should do) — Col. 3:16. It alone has life to the full (or should have) — Jn. 10:10. It has power over the devil, and it can heal the sick and raise the dead — Mk. 16:17, 18. It is God's property for it is built by God, "I will build My Church" — Mt. 16:18; and it is God Who adds members to His Church — Acts 2:47.

Since the Church is clearly a supernatural body we should not be too surprised if we find in scripture a type of government which is unnatural and which expresses God's 'foolishness' rather than man's wisdom. Jesus said many surprising things, e.g. "Blessed are the meek, for they shall inherit the earth". — Mt. 5:5; and when the apostles were discussing who should be accounted the greatest among them, Jesus gave them a surprising answer. The occasion was after He had established the Lord's Supper and just before He was to be crucified. It was an appropriate occasion for Him to say, "I want you, Peter (or whoever), to be in charge after I am gone". But He did no such thing; on the contrary He said, "The Kings of the Gentiles exercise lordship over them; and they that exercise authority upon them are called benefactors. But ye shall not be so: but he that is greatest among you, let him be as the younger; and he that is chief, as he that doth serve". — Lk. 22:25, 26; Mk. 10:42—44; Mt. 20:25—28. This is amazing, the apostles were instructed that no-one should exercise lordship nor kingly authority over his fellow-believers. Lordship and kingly authority are out, and in are humility and meekness: the greatest to be as the younger and the chief as the servant. A characteristic of the younger is that he is more willing to learn — and more willing to submit to others. Not one forcing his views on others — not one strutting about like a lord all dolled-up in fine clothes, but one acting like a servant wearing, metaphorically, an apron. Dear reader, we must pause to meditate here, for we are about to receive two great shocks:—

Shock No.1: Jesus did not appoint anybody to take His place after He was crucified.

Shock No.2: The most able of the apostles was to be a learner, submitting himself to others and serving them.

We are face to face with God's foolishness which is wiser than men. We might think, 'But Jesus, every earthly organisation has somebody at the head?' I can imagine His reply, 'Yes, but the Church is not an earthly organisation; nevertheless it is going to have somebody in charge, somebody at the head, it will be Myself and none other, continually'. Josh. 1:5 and Heb. 13:5. "I will never leave thee, nor forsake thee". "Christ in you, the hope of glory". Col. 1:27b. "Ye are the temple of the living God; as God hath said, I will dwell in them, and walk in them; and I will be their God, and they shall be My people". 2 Cor. 6:16. "Behold, I stand at the door, and knock: if any man hear My voice, and open the door, I will come in to him, and sup with him, and he with Me". — Revn. 3:20.

There is plenty of evidence that the Lord Jesus lives in His Church: giving life, performing miracles, giving direction. So the Church has one person at the head, the Lord Jesus Christ, and no-one else can take His place — and no-one else should attempt to do so. Furthermore the greatest among us is to be as the younger; and the chief as he that doth serve. That puts us right down to lowest place. It tramples on all our superiority, all our pride. No longer can we boast about our education, nor about our achievements.

There is left only one person in whom we can glory and that is our wonderful, wonderful Saviour — Jesus our Lord, our only Lord.

This, of course, runs counter to human nature. The natural man, in general, likes to be boss and dictate to others and likes those over him to be "Kingly" and "Lordly"; well-educated, eloquent, well-dressed, and having a university degree . . . . perhaps in the hope that some of his earthly glory will fall on us! Ignorant and unlearned men such as Peter and John — Acts 4:13 — would not be our choice, in the flesh. But these men were able to do great things — through Jesus — who was dwelling in them; they had great power over sickness and over devils — Acts 3:6; — Lk. 10:17. When at Lystra, Paul healed a crippled man and caused a great stir — Acts 14:8—15, the people began to worship Paul and Barnabas, but the apostles were horrified. They told the people to turn from such vanities unto the living God. They, the apostles, refused their adulation and worship. The natural man loves adulation, and church leaders need to be aware of this; they should not revel in adulation; they should not love the praise of men more than the praise of God — Jn. 12:43.

One of man's greatest weakness is paying but scant attention to the Word of God. He does not hear it as often as he should; but even when he hears it, too often he does not let it sink deeply enough into him to be effective. Eve heard the Word of God about not eating a certain fruit. She remembered it, for she quoted it to the serpent. But it had not sunk deeply enough into her to save her from Satan's enticing and contradictory words. This study will bear fruit only if the scriptures sink deeply enough into you to result in obedience. It is amazing that not one of Jesus' disciples was expecting Him to rise from the grave despite His repeated statements to that coming event. No, not even His closest friends heard Him 'deeply' enough for His Word to bear fruit. The result was much needless sorrow.

We are warned against shallow hearing in — Dt. 28:1 where it says "Hearken diligently to the voice of the LORD our God to observe and to do all His commandments". There follows a comprehensive list of blessings and curses following obedience and disobedience. A wise man will take great notice of God's Word — Prov. 1:5. He will not lean to his own understanding — Prov. 3:5.

Have you, dear reader, been hearkening diligently? If so your heart should be ready for some more of God's "foolishness", which is wiser than men.

Chapter 3 — ELDERS — GOD CHOOSES THE RULERS

We turn to Acts 14:23 where we read, "When they (Paul and Barnabas) had ordained ELDERS in every church, and had prayed with fasting, they commended them to the Lord on whom they believed".

Barnabas and Saul had been sent out — by the Holy Ghost — to found churches in Asia — Acts 13:2. This they had done and now they were revisiting them to encourage the believers and they ORDAINED ELDERS IN EVERY CHURCH. It might be expected that they would have ordained one of the gifted men of Ephesians 4:11: apostles, prophets, evangelists, pastors, teachers. No, they ordained ELDERS — not a priest, not a vicar, not a minister, not a leader, not a pastor, but elders. Why elders? The name implies age; and age brings on loss of vigour and a tendency to be 'past it', out of date, lacking in enthusiasm for new ideas. Surely we need someone to lead the youth in all their activities; don't we need someone straight from college, who has lots of vigour and all the latest ideas for attracting people to the church? No, please God, not stuffy old elders!

But God replies, "I warned that My ways are not your ways, and that My "foolishness" is greater than your wisdom. The churches in Asia are to have ELDERS". So here we are facing:—

Shock No.3: Churches must have elders ordained in them.

Paul, later, sends for the elders of the Ephesian Church and exhorts them to, "take heed therefore unto yourselves, and to all the flock, over the which the Holy Ghost hath made you OVERSEERS, to feed the Church of God, which He hath purchased with His Own blood", Acts 20:28. Elders then, are the overseers, and it was the Holy Ghost Who gave them that office. It was not a brainwave of Paul but a deliberate act of the Holy Ghost. Additionally they are to feed the flock of God, the Church which

God purchased with His Own blood.

Shock No.4: These elders have prime responsibility. They are not there to assist the pastor, or whoever, but they are to be over everybody in the Church and they are given the responsibility of seeing that the Church is fed.

'Overseeing' implies taking responsibility for all that takes place in the Church: making sure that all the gifted men — of Eph. 4:11 — can exercise their gifts and bring about what is described in the next two verses, Eph. 4:12, 13 — "For the perfecting of the saints, for the work of the ministry, for the edifying of the Body of Christ: till we all come in the unity of the faith, and of the knowledge of the Son of God, unto a perfect man, unto the measure of the stature of the fulness of Christ". Now we see the function of these five gifted men: they are to minister their gifts so as to bring all in the Church to perfect men and women. Obviously they need the opportunity for exercising their particular gifts and this could not happen if one man was allowed to monopolise the platform or pulpit.

Shock No.5: We have got it all wrong when we appoint one man to do all the ministry. And if, in addition, we expect him to take the oversight of the church, then the error becomes even worse.

Dear reader, please hearken diligently, for on you falls the task of moving in line with the scriptures as and when opportunity affords!

Since elders have responsibility to feed the church as well as oversee it — Acts 20:28, it follows that they themselves will be concerned with ministering, they will use their ministry gifts; but their first responsibility is, I think, the overseeing of the church. There'll be others to minister, but it is only elders who have the oversight, and no-one else. Overseeing implies ruling; this is brought out in 1 Tim. 5:17, where Paul says, "Let the elders that rule well be counted worthy of double honour, especially they who labour in the word and doctrine". Elders are to be in the plural, there have to be several in each church, never one elder to a church. Why? We are not told, but I think it is to preserve adherence to the Word of God, and to preserve balance between the different ministries. If there were only one elder it would become easier for satan to lead the church astray, for it is easier to deceive one man than several united men. I wonder if 'modernism' would have achieved such a hold on the churches if they had each been ruled by several men: I think not!

That elders are to feed the flock of God and take the oversight of it is revealed also in — 1 Pet. 5:2. Peter was not only an apostle but also an elder, and he writes, "The elders, feed the flock of God which is among you, taking the oversight thereof, not by constraint, but willingly; not for filthy lucre, but of a ready mind; neither as being lords over God's heritage, but being ensamples unto the flock".

What does a well-fed flock look like? I suppose, full of spiritual life and vigour, bubbling over with joy and praise to our dear, dear Jesus Christ and to our all-wise God; intoxicated by love one for another; hardly able to walk for dancing; full of power to heal the sick and to deliver those oppressed by the devil; full of peace and faith. Ministry has to be not only to the head but right down into the spirit, where lives the Holy Ghost, and from whence comes power to work miracles. "The spirit of man is the candle of the LORD, searching all the inward parts of the belly" — Prov. 20:27. We need Bible knowledge, but also the life of the Spirit working in us. We need those who can minister life. Is it not now apparent that the Church needs the different ministries of Eph. 4:11 and that no one man alone has this capability?

Chapter 4 — SO GOD LAYS DOWN THE RULES

These are remarkable and reflect once more God's 'foolishness' which is wiser than men. The rules for elders are set out in 1 Tim. 3:2—7 and in Titus 1:5—9 and are listed below:—

1. Blameless.
2. Husband of one wife.
3. Vigilant.
4. Sober.
5. Of good behaviour.
6. Given to hospitality.
7. Apt to teach.
8. Not given to wine.
9. No striker.
10. Not greedy of filthy lucre.
11. Patient.
12. Not a brawler.
13. Not covetous.
14. One that ruleth well his own house.
15. Not a novice.
16. Having a good report from outsiders.
17. Not self-willed.
18. Not soon angry.
19. A lover of good men.
20. Just.
21. Holy.
22. Temperate.
23. Holding fast the faithful word.

Most of these concern character and only a few concern academic accomplishments. Characterwise, he is to be beyond reproach, but academically he could be a fisherman or a carpenter; he is required to be 'apt to teach', involving, of course, knowledge of the Bible, and he has to be able to rule his own house (No.14).

So **Shock No.6:** The overseers of the church do not need a college education nor a university degree! Furthermore a man straight from college or university could not be an elder because he would be but a novice (15) and may have no family in which he has proved his ruling ability (14).

Additionally, he may be so educated as to have rejected much of God's Word as fables; he may not believe in miracles nor the return of Christ, and hence he would fail to meet qualification No.23. If the local church was ruled by a multiplicity of elders it is unlikely that they would accept such a man into eldership, nor to minister in the church. That such do minister in the church today brings out the importance of adherence to God's Word on eldership. By departing from it we have enabled satan to have a field-day in making many churches powerless to bring about the second birth, let alone work miracles.

Hearken diligently!

Chapter 5 — AND THEN SEALS HIS CHOICE!

In the Old Testament the priests, and things set apart for the worship of God, all had to be anointed with a special anointing oil — Ex. 29:21, 29 and Ex. 30:25 +. The anointing represented consecration to the LORD, and symbolises the Holy Spirit in the New Testament. Whilst no ceremony of anointing is mentioned for elders, there is still spiritual anointing, which is spiritual empowering for their task. The capability of certain men in the church showed their suitabilty to be ordained as elders. They HAD the anointing of GOD on them. Jesus said, "The Spirit of the LORD is upon Me, because He hath anointed Me to preach the Gospel" — Lk. 4:18. Jesus had both the Holy Ghost and the anointing, and so do all of God's children when they are given a specific task by the Holy Ghost.

Chapter 6 — WHERE DO BISHOPS COME IN?

The first mention of bishops is in Philippians 1:1. Paul and Timotheus writing to the church in Philippi say, "To all the saints in Christ Jesus which are at Philippi, with the Bishops and Deacons". He does not here mention ELDERS. This is the first mention of bishops, and it seems strange that they should suddenly appear and equally strange that elders are not mentioned. The explanation of this mystery is very simple. In Titus 1:5 Paul speaks of elders and later, whilst obviously still speaking of the same people, he calls them bishops in verse 7. Hence bishops is merely an alternative name for elders; it is not a new group of people. In modern usage 'bishop' denotes something different, a lot different from elder. We don't find the word 'bishop' in the New International Version of the Bible. Instead, is used the word 'overseer' and thus it avoids confusion. Since 'elders' is by far the most frequently used name, it is suggested that we stay with it and drop the word bishop, especially as 'bishop' has such a different meaning in modern times.

Chapter 7 — AND WHATEVER IS THE PRESBYTERY?

This word apears but once in scripture where we read, "Neglect not the gift that is in thee, — by — the laying on of the hands of the PRESBYTERY" — 1 Tim. 4:14. This word appears suddenly in the context of an operation not new, the laying on of hands.

The Greek word for PRESBYTERY is PRESBUTERION and the Greek word for elder is PRESBUTEROS. Strong's Concordance presumes that presbuterion is derived from presbuteros, and that presbytery is merely another name for the elders. The New International Version, in place of presbytery puts "the body of the elders".

So, to avoid confusion we should stick to elders and drop both bishop and presbytery. Some people will not like us doing this! But never mind. We are required by scripture to "all speak the same thing, and that there be no divisions among you; but that ye be perfectly joined together in the same mind and in the same judgement" — 1 Cor. 1:10. It helps if we all use the same names, for then it is easier for us to communicate with one another. The more we move towards scripture, the more we shall destroy the differences between various church groups, and the easier it will be to become a unity, THAT unity for which Jesus prayed in John 17. It is a cause for rejoicing that the denominational barriers are more frequently being ignored in these days than in earlier days. Certainly sectarianism is decried in Mk. 9:38, 39.

Chapter 8 — BUT WHO CHOOSES THE DEACONS?

We read about them first in Acts chapter 6. There was murmuring in the church because some widows were being neglected 'in the daily ministration'. This, presumably, was in financial help. The twelve apostles corrected the situation by appointing seven good men to take care of it, saying, "It is unreasonable for us to leave the Word of God to serve tables. We will give ourselves continually to prayer and the ministry of the Word" — Acts 6:1—4. It is important to note how the apostles guarded their time of prayer and the ministry of the Word; and how ready they were to delegate authority to others. I think we often fail in both these respects, and we need to learn to concentrate our efforts on our own particular job, avoiding distractions. Have you noticed that neither Jesus nor Paul did much in the way of baptising? Could this not be because others could do it equally well? How we rush about from one thing to another these days! Why? There is no need!

It is, I think, interesting that the apostles left the choosing of the deacons to the disciples. They gave the disciples a job to do, and then the apostles made their choice official by appointing them after prayer and the laying on of the apostles' hands — Acts 6:6. The names of these first deacons are recorded in verse 5, and they include Stephen, a man of great spirituality.

The qualifications for deacons are given in Acts 6:3 and in 1 Tim. 3:8—12. They are similar to those given for elders and require a very high standard of character, but we will list them out:—

1. Of honest report.
2. Full of the Holy Ghost and wisdom.
3. Grave.
4. Not double-tongued.
5. Not given to much wine.
6. Not greedy of filthy lucre.
7. Holding the mystery of the faith in a pure conscience.
8. Blameless.
9. Having grave wives.
10. Having not slanderous wives.
11. Having sober wives.
12. The husband of one wife.
13. Ruling their children and houses well.

"For they that have used the office of a deacon well purchase to themselves a good degree, and great boldness in the faith which is in Christ Jesus" — 1 Tim. 3:13.

Stephen was full of faith and power and did great wonders and miracles among the people — Acts 6:8. Although the deacon's special function was to relieve elders for prayer and the ministry of the Word, they, in common with the elders and the gifted men of Eph. 4:11, were given liberty to preach. It was the gifts that gave this liberty and not the office, if any.

In the Revised Standard Version of the Bible, Phoebe, a woman, is called a deaconess — Rom. 16:1.

Chapter 9 — APOSTLES, GOD'S PIONEER PLANTERS

Initially they were the twelve disciples whom Jesus chose to be with Him in His ministry — Mt. 10:2. But others were added to them in the course of time. Paul and Barnabas were added — Acts 13:2, 4. And Andronicus and Junia are mentioned as "apostles of note" in Rom. 16:7. The implication is that there were others, though not of note. The apostles Paul and Barnabas were separated by the Holy Ghost from the church in Antioch for "the work of founding new churches in Asia". They remained in these churches only long enough to establish them, then they ordained ELDERS to look after them; to take on the oversight and feeding. They did not ordain apostles or anybody else for the oversight. Similarly Titus was given the task of appointing elders in every city, not apostles.

The function of APOSTLES would appear to be the establishing of new churches, which later are to be looked after by elders. Presumably to free the apostles to establish more new churches. The functions of apostles and elders are therefore different, but a man may be qualified for both tasks. Peter was such — 1 Pet. 1:1 and 5:1. There is no indication that the oversight of a local church is given to anybody but elders when once it is established. Apostles therefore visiting a church which had been "passed over" to elders would, it would seem, have to abide under the authority of the elders. But of course the apostles would receive much respect in these circumstances.

Our modern name for the function of establishing new churches is "missionary work". This is not a scriptural name. It seems that we should be sending out apostles to found churches!

(It is probably worth mentioning here, that the Greek word "Apostolos", from which obviously the English word 'apostle' is simply a translation, and which only appears in the New Testament, means "one sent forth" — and just that!   *A.B.*)

Chapter 10 — PASTORS, THE CARING UNDER-SHEPHERDS

The name implies caring for God's children, as a shepherd cares for his sheep. There is however a great difference in the amount of time it takes to perform these tasks. Sheep have instincts enabling them to live with but little attention. They know how to feed themselves, what to run away from, and their clothes grow naturally. One man can look after about 500 sheep. With God's children it's different, they need to be fed by others all their life, and sometimes need coaxing to get them to take their food (the Word). Their clothes don't come naturally and they have to be dressed by others in suitable garments (humility). They get into all sorts of scrapes (sin). They stop breathing sometimes (prayer). But, oh! they become so wonderfully beautiful when properly cared for (pastored). Jesus was our example and He was able to look after twelve of these precious things. How many can you look after? 500? No! — not even 12. I have mentioned only a few of the duties of pastoring; e.g. there is a need for keeping warm, cuddling (love). There is a need for the exercise of spiritual muscles (witnessing, etc.), they have to be taken sometimes to the doctor (the special preacher or conference); and so we could go on. I am convinced that churches need in them a whole multitude of pastors, and that the chief reason for many Christians being weak is lack of personal pastors!

In scripture, do we find a pastor at the head of a church? No, elders in the plural should be at the head, and there should be as many pastors under them as it takes to do the job of pastoring the whole church. Of course, all the other gifted men mentioned in Eph. 4:11 are contributing in caring.

Chapter 11 — AUTHORITY OVER THE LOCAL CHURCH

For a long time most local churches have obeyed some human authority over them. These authorities have issued service books telling the local church what to say, when to say it, and what to pray; and to some extent dictate the doctrine. The scriptures have come to be regarded as of lesser importance than the "service" book. Many churches, of course, have rejected this system and have the word 'free' in their title, like Free Evangelical. Our task is to determine, if we can, whether churches should be directed from a higher human authority or be free of such direction altogether, according to scripture.

We have in scripture a number of letters written to churches by one of its founders — Paul. In general these letters set out to provide helpful guidance rather than to dictate details such as appear in our prayer book. Paul was given much revelation from God, and much of what he wrote was new. If anybody had a right to dictate to local churches it would be Paul. But Paul does not take a dictatorial attitude, but rather as one among his brethren. He often writes, "I beseech you —" and rarely, if ever, "I command you --". In the first verse of 2 Cor. 10 he writes, "Now I Paul myself beseech you by the meekness and gentleness of Christ, who in presence am base among you, but being absent am bold toward you: But I beseech you --".

James once made a speech in the presence of Paul and Barnabas in which he says, "My sentence is that --". Acts 15:19. The occasion was when Paul and Barnabas went up from Antioch to Jerusalem to discuss the dissension which had arisen over circumcision. James gives his judgement on the matter. Some have thought that this proves that the Jerusalem church had authority over the church at Antioch. But is this not reading too much into the incident? Is it not only natural for one church to consult with another when difficulty arises? Surely it does not follow necessarily that one has authority over the other. I know of no scripture which clearly supports authority external to a local church. Each local church has over the elders the Lord Jesus Christ, and Him alone.

Much of what we see amiss in some denominations seems to have been passed on from 'Headquarters', but it is not the purpose of this study to go into that. However, one wonders if the churches would not be better served if they had only the scriptures for doctrine and only the elders to take on the oversight.

Chapter 12 — GOD'S GIFTS TO THE CHURCH

Mention has been made already of the five different kinds of gifted people listed in Eph. 4:11; apostles, prophets, evangelists, pastors, teachers. The next verses, 12 and 13, tell us why they are given to the church:— ''For the perfecting of the saints, for the work of the ministry, for the edifying of the body of Christ: till we all come in the unity of the faith, and of the knowledge of the Son of God, unto a perfect man, unto the measure of the stature of the fulness of Christ''. It is self-evident that all these gifts must be in operation, and that it falls on the shoulders of the elders to ensure that no one gifted person takes up more than their proper share of the time available. There will, I suppose, always be some more loquacious than others!

Besides these five gifted saints with their differing ministries, the church has also been given the benefit of nine spiritual gifts outlined in 1 Cor. 12:7—11. These are manifested by the Holy Ghost, using whom He will, when He will. It is not man controlling the exercise of these gifts, but the Holy Ghost. It is needful then for the Holy Ghost to be given the opportunity to operate. We should not over-organise our meetings. The nine gifts are:—

1. Wisdom.
2. Knowledge.
3. Faith.
4. Healings.
5. Miracles.
6. Prophesy.
7. Discerning of spirits.
8. Tongues.
9. Interpretation of Tongues.

Past experience in many churches has been that there is no manifestation of these gifts of the Spirit, and the conclusion reached has been that gifts belonged only to a past age. But this of course is erroneous because the gifts are still being manifested in other churches.

Furthermore, each church member has differing gifts, according to the grace that is given to us. Rom. 12:6—8:—

1. Prophecy, let us prophesy according to the proportion of faith.
2. Ministry, let us wait on our ministry.   (wait:— attend to,
3. Teaching, let us wait on our teaching.   remain at, serve
4. Exhortation, let us wait on our exhortation.   as attendant to--)
5. Giving, let us do it with simplicity.   *(Chambers' dict.)*
6. Ruling, let us do it with diligence.
7. Mercy, let us show it with cheerfulness.

The list of gifts mentioned in all three places — Eph. 4, Rom. 12 and 1 Cor. 12 — are probably intended to be representative rather than exhaustive. For example, there is no mention of 'encouraging'.

It is a matter of great rejoicing that, in recent times, more and more saints are being filled with the Holy Ghost, baptised in the Spirit, and manifesting the spiritual gifts. They have a freedom and vigour in praising God, previously unknown to them. It is sad that some Christians misunderstand what is happening when saints become filled with the Spirit. They think they have become unbalanced, when they see them throwing their arms in the air and getting all excited and loving one another and kissing one another and dancing about. But rest assured, they are quite sane — just bubbling over with the joy that God has put inside them. As the return of Jesus draws nearer and nearer it seems that the church gets livelier and livelier. Covet earnestly the best gifts, 1 Cor. 12:31.

Chapter 13 — SHOULD THERE BE 'LEADERS'?

Moses is an example of a man chosen by God to lead people. He was to lead the children of Israel out of Egypt into the promised land. This was not only a difficult assignment, but humanly speaking, an impossible assignment; for Pharaoh was not the type of man to be easily persuaded to give up his slaves, and furthermore the journey to the promised land was fraught with insuperable difficulties. We might think it would require a Super man. God thought it required a man lacking in eloquence, slow of tongue (Ex. 4:10) and so lacking in strong, aggressive personality as to be described as "very meek above all men which are upon the face of the earth" — Num. 12:3. Now who is going to accept that kind of leadership? Surely nobody! So once again we see God's 'foolishness' which is wiser than men!

So **Shock No.7:** is God choosing, for a difficult leadership role, — a man totally lacking in basic leadership qualities!

We need to think about how the assignment worked out! Poor Moses needed to have some assurance from God, and God gave it to him by enabling him to perform miracles: by turning Moses' rod into a serpent and then back again into a rod — Ex. 4:3—4. And then God told Moses to put his hand into his bosom, that it might immediately turn leprous, and on inserting it into his bosom a second time it became well again. God gave assurance by a demonstration of the miraculous. The whole assignment was to be bathed in miracles worked by God through an instrument that would carry out God's instructions. Moses did not need to be clever, but he did need to hear God's Word and obey it. God was going to supply all the needed miraculous power. Praise God! Moses was obedient and the assignment was successful, except that the Israelites' faith was too weak for them to march into the land of promise; but this does not reflect on Moses' enablement. Moses had all that was needed, because he had God.

In the list of qualifications for elders, there is no mention of leadership qualities; eloquence, or strong personality. In the list of gifted men, in Eph. 4:11, there is no mention of leaders. Similarly in Rom. 12:6—8 the list of gifts does not include leadership, although it does include ruling. The gifts of the Spirit in 1 Cor. 12 do not include leadership qualities like eloquence or personality. Jesus taught us that, "Blessed are the meek: for they shall inherit the earth" — Mt. 5:5. So, there is a future for the meek people, they shall inherit the earth. Let us go back to the garden of Eden, where we learn so much that is basic truth. God dictated what may be eaten and what was forbidden. He, God, intended to be the leader. But satan set about snatching the leadership out of God's hands by pouring enticing words into Eve's ears. Adam and Eve had a choice to make: either they could obey God or enjoy for a season the benefits of disobedience. You and I are faced with a similar situation. We can either obey God's Word, the Bible; or we can eclipse God's Word and follow man, influenced by satan.

In the scriptures we find surprisingly little use of the word "leader". It is missing entirely from the New Testament, and it appears only four times in the Old Testament. "Leaders" in the plural appears but three times in the Old Testament and only once in the New, where it speaks of blind leaders of the blind — Mt. 15:14. The word "lead" appears thirteen times in the New Testament, but never once does it support human leadership in the church. No, not even once!

Shock No.8: No direct mention of human christian leaders in the church, in the New Testament.

Paul, speaking of his power, says, "Have we not power to lead about a sister, a wife, as well as other apostles etc.". He is saying he has power to lead, but he is not actually advocating the use of that power — 1 Cor. 9:5. Rather he is setting out to argue his status and entitlement to recognition for reward — v.11.

There is, of course, a sense in which much of the ministry results in "leading". But that is different from presenting our own bright ideas, having no scriptural basis.

God sometimes calls a person with natural gifts like eloquence and a higher intelligence. But it is, perhaps, harder for such to believe in the miracles and in God's "foolishness", rather than in man's wisdom. In particular, it is perhaps harder for the intelligent to bow to God's Word and let the Holy Spirit do the leading.

Chapter 14 — THE PLACE OF WOMEN ----

There is a wide difference of belief on this subject: some people believing that in public worship women have equal rights to men; whilst others believe that women should be silent. The difference indicates that great care should be taken when interpreting relevant scriptures. It is all too easy to quote scriptures supporting, (or seeming to support) our own belief whilst ignoring those which oppose our belief. It is also all too easy to read into a scripture more than it says. An attempt is being made here to avoid these errors and to present a worthwhile and balanced judgement after much study, meditation and prayer. The subject is very important because about half of the church consists of women.

We will establish first the basic capability of women, and then go on to establish any restrictions to their sphere of ministry. It is written, "For as many of you as have been baptised into Christ have put on Christ. There is neither Jew nor Greek, there is neither bond nor free, there is neither male nor female: for ye are all one in Christ" — Gal. 3:27—28. Hence 'in Christ' there is no distinction: males and females are one! They both equally form temples in which Christ dwells and in which He shows His glory. "Christ in you, the hope of glory" — Col. 1:27b. On the day of Pentecost both men and women continued in prayer in the upper room — Acts 1:14, "they were all filled with the Holy Ghost, and began to speak with other tongues, as the Spirit gave them utterance". Acts 2:4.

Peter, explaining what had happened at Pentecost says, "This is that which was spoken by the prophet Joel; and it shall come to pass in the last days, saith God, I will pour out of My Spirit upon all flesh: and your sons and daughters shall prophesy (etc.)" — Acts 2:16—17.

Here again no distinction is made between man and woman;

33

c

both were filled with the Holy Ghost, both spoke in other tongues and both prophesied. It is also our experience today that this equality of basic capability is being demonstrated.

We now come to any restrictions in ministry by women. A notable scripture is, "I suffer not a woman to teach, nor to usurp authority over the man, but to be in silence". 1 Tim. 2:12. Another notable scripture is, "Let your women keep silence in the churches: for it is not permitted unto them to speak; but they are commanded to be under obedience, as also says the law". — 1 Cor. 14:34. These two scriptures might seem to remove completely any possibility for women to take part audibly in church.

One requires women to be "in silence" and the other requires them to 'keep silence'. For many saints these two scriptures show that there is no place for women to minister in church. Nevertheless, it is customary for women to be allowed to join the men in singing, in repeating part of a set service, including reciting a creed. So there seems to be a common consent that women may take at least a restricted audible part and therefore are not to be in silence all the time. Either "common consent" is at fault by not keeping women "silent", or the interpretation of the command to silence is wrong. We shall re-examine our interpretation very carefully a little later, but first we will look at the specific things associated with 'silence'. In 1 Tim. 2:12 there is specific mention of teaching and usurping authority over man as being prohibited, and in fact it would seem that the required silence stems from the need to maintain the authority of the man over woman. There are a number of scriptures showing that man has been given this authority over women. For example, "The husband is the head of the wife, even as Christ is the head of the church" — Eph. 5:23. "Ye wives, be in subjection to your own husbands" — 1 Pet. 3:1a. "It is not good that the man should be alone; I will make him an help-meet (suitable) for him" — Gen. 2:18. "And thy (Eve's) desire shall be to thy husband, and he shall rule over thee". — Gen. 3:16b. Hence men and women, though not different spiritually, do have different functions. They complement each other with the man being the head, and this difference is to be observed in church by women refraining from teaching and usurping authority over men.

Regarding the requirement for women to be in silence, we will study this in connection with 1 Cor. 14 where the whole chapter is concerned with regulating the ministry to ensure that, "All things be done decently and in order" — v.40; "and be done unto edifying" — v.26. Verse 34 says, "Let your women keep silence in the churches: for it not permitted unto them to speak; but they are commanded to be under obedience, as also saith the law''. Verse 35 goes on to say, ''And if they will learn anything, let them ask their husbands at home: for it is a shame for women to speak in the church''. The women should, then, ask their questions of their husbands at home and not in the church. Why not? It would hardly be a matter of usurping the authority of the husband, for on the contrary it would rather show recognition of the husband being the head. We must look for another reason for the women not asking questions in church, and of course we immediately realise that asking questions could cause an interruption in the proceedings, and if many women were doing it there would be such a commotion that it would be difficult to hear the speaker and that would indeed be ''shameful''. It is difficult to imagine such a high level of talking in England, but in the Mediterranean countries the people are more excitable, and much more voluble.

It is suggested then, that the command for ''silence'' is at least associated with women asking questions, and is not necessarily to subdue women from taking part in the proceedings audibly, and that singing etc. may be in order.

We will now expand our vision somewhat by looking at other scriptures. In the same chapter, 1 Cor. 14:5 we read, ''I would that ye all spake with tongues, but rather that ye prophesied''. 'All' must mean both men and women. In verses 23—24 we again find the word 'all' used in connection with speaking in tongues and prophesying. In verse 31 once more, ''For ye may 'all' prophesy one by one, etc.''. We are now left in no doubt whatever that women may speak in tongues and prophesy and that the command for women to be 'silent' in church cannot apply to tongues and prophecy. There seems no reason, then, why it should apply to the remaining seven gifts of the Spirit mentioned in 1 Cor. 12:7—11. However in order to maintain authority of the man, a woman should not teach as this would be usurping authority. Preaching usually involves a big element of teaching and would therefore be forbidden.

This brings us to consider head coverings, and their purpose. Perhaps some who do cover their heads do so without knowing why, apart from its being a custom. It is written, ''But every woman that prayeth or prophesieth with her head uncovered dishonoureth her head: for that is even all one as if she were shaven. For if the woman be not covered, let her also be shorn: but if it be a shame for a woman to be shorn or shaven, let her be covered'' — 1 Cor. 11:5—6. The reason for head covering goes right back to creation. ''Neither was the man created for the woman; but the woman for the man'' — 1 Cor. 11:9. The purpose of the head covering then is to symbolise that the man is the head of the woman. The scripture gives a second reason for the woman covering her head, and that is because of the angels — 1 Cor. 11:10. In church we "are come unto an innumerable company of angels" — Heb. 12:22. The teaching on the need for women to cover their heads is not always well received. To avoid discord, the scripture has some comforting words, "If any man seem to be contentious, we have no such custom, neither the churches of God" — 1 Cor. 11:16. Some modern versions give exactly the reverse of this: instead of "no such custom", they say "no other practice".

Summarising Chapter 14
Spiritually there is no difference between men and women; the Holy Ghost empowers both equally; and both have equal liberty to minister their gifts in the church audibly. But women should normally refrain from teaching, where this could be construed as usurping authority over men, and they should cover their heads in recognition of the headship of men.

Everything should be done decently and in order, the ministry is to be by course, one person at a time, the others being in silence. Women and men should not ask questions in church but to keep silence whilst another is ministering. Ruling and 'overseeing' the church is the function of men rather than women, normally.

It is salutary to remember that the rapid growth of a church in South Korea was due largely to evangelisation by women. We need to question whether in UK we have made full use of women's capabilities either in the church or out of it. Have we not too often so 'silenced' our women that they have no freedom in the church to minister their spiritual gifts?

Chapter 15 — THE HEAD OF THE CHURCH

Jesus is a perfect gentleman, He never thrusts Himself upon us. He has no place in the church unless we want Him to come in and revolutionise us. He is all — or nothing. His rightful place in the church is at the head, over the elders. The Church is His, He bought it at a great price; He loves it; He adds to it; He dwells in it; He walks in it; He is our God and we are His people — 2 Cor. 6:16.

We may 'posh up' the church building and have a fine organ: but I tell you it is Jesus who 'poshes up' people and causes them to produce sweet music in His ears! It is Jesus who gives life and light, not man. We may strut about in fine clothes like peacocks, but face to face with Jesus our fine clothes are but dirty rags, and our pride becomes our shame. "He that glorieth, let him glory in the LORD" — 1 Cor. 1:31.

Jesus instructs by His written Word so that the Church can become the light of the world, but only Jesus can be a Lord in the church — not man — 1 Pet. 5:3. Man is not even permitted to be a master in the church, for it is written, "Be ye not called Rabbi: for one is your Master, even Christ; and all ye are brethren. And call no man your 'father' upon the earth: for one is your Father, which is in heaven. Neither be ye called 'masters': for one is your Master, even Christ". — Mt. 23:8—10. The next verse (11) tells us what the greatest among us should be; he should be our servant. Not much scope here for self-glorification! no, the church is for the glorification of its Lord. We are His friends if we do whatsoever He commands us — Jn. 15:14.

Chapter 16 — THE DESIGNER'S INSTRUCTION MANUAL

Colossians 3:16 says "Let the word of Christ dwell in you richly in all wisdom; teaching and admonishing one another in psalms and hymns and spiritual songs, singing with grace in your hearts to the Lord". Note, it says teaching and admonishing one another, and this instruction is given to the whole church at Colosse who are to have the "word of Christ dwelling in them richly in all wisdom". It is not given solely to the elders.

Do we, nowadays, expect the members of our local church to be teaching and admonishing one another? Or do we expect the teaching and admonishing to come from just one or two men frequently known as The Minister, The Priest, The Pastor, or The Clergy? And, we might ask, are the remainder of our church members capable of teaching and admonishing one another? Also, is it necessary for the church members to teach and admonish one another? Is this some more of God's 'foolishness' which is wiser than men? Yes it is:—

Shock No.9:   The church members should teach and admonish one another!

We have seen already in chapter 3, headed 'ELDERS — GOD CHOOSES THE RULERS', that the responsibility for feeding the church should not rest on one man; Acts 20:28, and that the church, for its perfection, needs ministry from a multiplicity of men having differing spiritual gifts; Eph. 4:11—13. Paul, writing to the Romans says "and I myself also am persuaded of you, my brethren, that ye also are full of goodness, filled with all knowledge, able also to admonish one another" — Romans 15:14.

Peter writing to the strangers scattered throughout Pontus, Galatia, Cappadocia, Asia, and Bithynia, says, "As every man hath received the gift, even so minister the same one to another, as good stewards of the manifold grace of God" — 1 Pet. 4:10. Paul said, "Having then gifts differing according to the grace that is given us, whether prophecy, let us prophesy according to the proportion of faith: or ministry, let us wait on our ministering; or he that teacheth, on teaching; or he that exhorteth, on exhortation" — Romans 12:6—8. In another letter Paul mentions the manifestation of nine differing spiritual gifts, divided to every man "severally as he (The Holy Spirit) will" — 1 Cor. 12:7—11. Note, it says 'every' man; and earlier, in verse 7, we read that the manifestation of the Spirit is given to every man. In 1 Cor. 14:12 we read, "forasmuch as ye are zealous of spiritual gifts, seek that ye may excel to the edifying of the church". So, the edification of the church involves the manifestation of various spiritual gifts which are given to every man "severally as as He will".

1 Cor. 12:25 says, "That there should be no schism in the body; but that the members should have the same care one for another". Note the 'same care' — in contrast to the notion that the care of the body rests with just a few men, or one man! Hebrews 10:25 says, "Not forsaking the assembling of ourselves together, as the manner of some is; but exhorting one another: and so much the more as ye see the day approaching". Hebrews 3:13 says, "But exhort one another daily, while it is called Today; lest any of you be hardened through the deceitfulness of sin". 1 Cor. 14:31 says, "For ye may all prophecy one by one, that all may learn, and all may be comforted".

All these scriptures combine to tell us that we should minister to (teach, exhort etc.) one another, in contrast to the commonly accepted idea that the ministry should come from the 'ordained' man at the top. It may come as a surprise to some of my readers, that all born-again church members have BEEN ordained by God. John 15:16 says, "ye have not chosen me, but I (Jesus) have chosen you, and ORDAINED you, that ye should go and bring forth fruit, and that your fruit should remain; that whatsoever ye shall ask of the Father in my name, He may give it you". So all true believers have been ordained by Jesus no matter which church they are in, no matter whether they be male or female or whether they be young or old. There is no need to debate whether or not women may be ordained for the ministry, because God has already done the ordaining! Also, we do not need to make men priests, because God has already done that! 1 Peter 2:9 says "But ye are a chosen generation, a royal priesthood, an holy nation, a peculiar people; that ye should shew forth the praises of him who hath called you out of darkness into his marvellous light". Also in Revelation 1:6 we read, "and hath made us kings and priests unto God and his

(Jesus') Father; to him be glory and dominion for ever and ever. Amen".

Doubtless it is going to be very hard for most of us to accept such revolutionary teaching, but dear reader, if you are born-again you have the Spirit of God dwelling in you, and his function is to "Teach you all things, and bring all things to your remembrance, whatsoever I (Jesus) have said unto you". — John 14:26b. All we need is a willing heart to receive what He says, in the 'scriptures of truth'. In chapter 2, we saw who was to be the 'chief' in the church and the greatest. He was to be as a servant and as the youngest.

Obviously God has poured down blessing upon some churches where there is one man at the head and where there is little or no mutual ministry. But some churches have had to close through lack of support, and we do well to question the reason for the lack of support. Is it due to lack of supernatural power? Which in turn is due to lack of belief in all the scriptures? Man's wisdom cannot equal God's 'foolishness'. The author has had experience of attending churches regularly for many years without even knowing that there was such a thing as conversion, being born-again. He held all sorts of offices in the church, but had not been 'saved', to use a Bible expression, Acts 16:30. Teaching on the way of salvation either had been missing or insufficiently emphasied. This experience is all too common and terribly serious because the word of God says in Matt. 18:3, "Verily I say unto you, except ye be converted, and become as little children, ye shall not enter into the kingdom of heaven". Also in John 3:7 we read, "ye must be born again".

The effect of curtailing the ministry to the efforts of one man must be to curtail the ministry given, because no one man has all the knowledge needed, nor all the faith needed, nor all the ability needed. But even supposing there were such men, do not the saints (ordinary church members) need opportunity to minister their gifts in order to grow spiritually? To become "strong in the Lord, and in the power of His might?" Ephesians 6:10.

It is customary for us to put much stress on eloquent preaching, rather than on the working of miracles. In 1 Cor. 4:19—20, Paul says, "But I will come to you shortly, if the Lord will, and will know, not the speech of them which are puffed up, but the power. For the kingdom of God is not in word, but in power". The first disciples, of course, were told to wait in Jerusalem until they were baptised with the Holy Ghost; Acts 1:4—5; and that they would receive power after that the Holy Ghost had come upon them — Acts 1:8. In Acts 9:33—35 we read of the consequence of the healing of Aeneas by Peter: two whole towns turned to the Lord!

Shock No.10: The Kingdom of God is not in word, but in power!

The manner of ministry according to scripture, then, requires a manifestation of power; a recognition of the priesthood of all believers and freedom for mutual ministry. "Where the Spirit of the Lord is, there is liberty". 2 Cor. 3:17. We don't have to make liberty; we have merely to cease from opposing it!

A word of caution! Any enthusiasm we may have for making our own local church more scriptural may require us to have supernatural love and patience, and to be under the guidance of the Holy Ghost; all of which are available, Praise the Lord!

Chapter 17 — CONCLUSION TO PART 1

The writer has tried to present an accurate picture of scriptural teaching on the design and operation of 'Today's Church', but should you spot any errors or deficiencies, he asks for your forgiveness.

Many will find this study challenging, and worrying. It removes man from any exalted position. It encourages self-humiliation — Jas. 4:10; 1 Pet. 5:5. But these particular scriptures also speak of being lifted up by God and of being given grace. So dear reader take courage as you step out in obedience to God's Word, and God bless you.

"Study to show thyself approved unto God, a workman that needeth not to be ashamed, rightly dividing the word of truth". 2 Tim. 2:15.

Jesus said (to His Father), "Sanctify them through thy truth: thy word is truth". John 17:17.

(In the next part, we see the struggles and successes of the author as he, and later his family and friends, endeavour to learn and apply the design criteria God has specified for 'Today's Church', in His own word, the Bible. *A.B.*)

Part 2

THE AUTHOR'S EXPERIENCES

Chapter 18 — INTRODUCTION

After completing part 1, and presenting so many shocks, and so much unusual doctrinal matter, it only seemed right, desirable and fair, for me to present also some of my experiences. These are not confined to one type of denomination.

A sense of loyalty to a denomination, plus a natural and common belief that one's own denomination is the best, gives no encouragement for one to explore what is happening in other denominations. Consequently, there is a general lack of desire to heal the divisions between various sections of Christ's Church; although it would seem that there is in recent years more desire for unity than there used to be.

Unity of belief requires, does it not, common ground for that belief. The Holy Scriptures are common ground. If we all decide to follow the scriptures, come what may, we would have one foot on the ladder that leads to unity. The Bible says, "Ye are my friends if ye do whatsoever I command you". John 15:14.

You will be reading of some of the author's experiences of miracles which, hopefully, you will find encouraging and helpful in the destruction of the devilish theory that miracles, apart from conversion, ended with the first century.

Chapter 19 — THE AUTHOR'S CAPABILITIES

The author is a man of but mediocre capabilities, with a poor memory; who can't spell for toffee; who failed to pass the London Matriculation exams; who can't learn foreign languages except for a few words of French after much effort — *"Je ne parl pas francaise tres bien!"* And who couldn't sing in tune for most of his life. Put another way, I could sing only my own original tunes! But God has graciously helped me, so that now I can often sing at the top of my voice without being in fear of having a dig in the ribs by my neighbour as in former days.

How come then that a man with such mediocre capabilities should presume to teach others much more capable than himself? It is really not me doing the teaching, but rather it is the word of God that is doing the teaching. I am merely releasing the word of God and pointing out departures from it!

Have you noticed that Paul, in 1 Corinthians 1, tells us that "not many wise men after the flesh, not many mighty, not many noble, are called: But God hath chosen the foolish things of the world to confound the wise; and God hath chosen the weak things of the world to confound the things which are mighty; and base things of the world, and things which are despised, hath God chosen, yea, and things which are not, to bring to nought things that are: THAT NO FLESH SHOULD GLORY IN HIS PRESENCE". 1 Cor. 1:26—28.

The author would be the most uninteresting person in existence, but for one fact — the fact that God came into his life and performed miracles!

Chapter 20 — TITLES

It is common practice to give to the man leading a modern church the title of REVEREND. But in scripture no man is ever given that title. It never speaks of Reverend Peter or Reverend Paul. Indeed the word Reverend occurs but once and then it is applied to God, and not to man. Ps. 111:9.

Shock No.11:   If we would be true to scripture, we shall have to apply the title Reverend only to God and never to man, not even to great men like Paul.

Yes, it is quite right to respect our fellow christians and to submit ourselves to them. 1 Pet. 5:5 says — "Yea, all of you be subject one to another, and be clothed with humility: for God resisteth the proud, and giveth grace to the humble". We need to avoid worshipping man, which really amounts to idolatory.

Not only are we to avoid applying the title Reverend to man, but we are also to avoid applying even the title Father or Master, in a spiritual connection, to man. For the scripture says:—

"CALL NO MAN YOUR FATHER UPON THE EARTH, FOR ONE IS YOUR FATHER, WHICH IS IN HEAVEN. NEITHER BE YE CALLED MASTERS: FOR ONE IS YOUR MASTER, EVEN CHRIST." Matt. 23:9 & 10.

Even the Douai Version of the Bible translated from the Latin Vulgate and, I believe, favoured by Roman Catholics, says the same thing:— "And call none your father upon earth: for one is your father, who is in heaven". We need always to distinguish very clearly between what the scripture says and what has become customary, but is nevertheless contradictory to scripture! Jesus warned the Pharisees and the Scribes against making the word of God of none effect through their tradition. Mark 7:13. "Whoever exalteth himself shall be abased; and he that humbleth himself shall be exalted". Luke 14:11.

After washing the disciples' feet, Jesus said, "Ye also ought to wash one another's feet. For I have given you an example, that ye should do as I have done to you". John 13:14, 15.

There is much in the scriptures exhorting us to be humble — humility is a very hard lesson, but if we would be true followers of Jesus, there is no escaping it.

Chapter 21 — EDUCATION AND TESTIMONY

I left high school when I was only half-way through a four-year course because I wanted to be an engineer and I thought that Greek mythology, dates of kings and battles, and Shakespeare's plays to be a bit irrelevant to engineering.

I would go to church occasionally, but not regularly. At the age of eighteen I fell in love with a girl who had been an acquaintance for several years. Feeling ignorant, I went back to school again at West Ham Technical College. But I failed London Matriculation exam in English and French and, consequently, I could not obtain a degree in engineering.

My fiancée was a regular church attender and she wanted me to become a full member of the church. I decided that she was well worth that and so I was baptized and confirmed. Unfortunately, I did not understand what was meant by regeneration and I did not have the sense to ask. So it was not until many years later that I was converted, born-again and rebaptized.

When I was about 20, I left home to pursue my engineering career in Liverpool. After changing my lodgings several times, I settled down in a district with a rather 'posh' church in it. It had a fine organ, a paid choir and rented pews. The churchwardens were high up in the commercial world and often away from church on business. I had become the rector's right-hand man and I had to function sometimes in their place. I enjoyed marching up the aisle proudly carrying the collection plate. I had been on the Church Council for some years and I was rural deaconal representative, secretary of the free-will offering fund and on the finance committee. Also a sidesman and leader of the Youth Fellowship. But I was still unconverted and still quite ignorant of the existence of such a vital experience, without which no-one shall enter into the kingdom of heaven, Matt. 18:3, where Jesus said, "Verily I say

D

unto you, 'Except ye be converted, and become as little children, ye shall not enter into the Kingdom of Heaven' ''.

However, one day, whilst praying by my bedside, I was led to think about the words in the hymn — "There is a green hill far away, outside a city wall", and to face up to the words "There was no other good enough to pay the price of sin, He only could unlock the gate of heaven, and let us in". I had believed that Jesus died for the sins of the whole world, but now to think of Jesus dying in my place for my sin was quite a different matter. I told God that I didn't understand it, "but if it is true that Jesus died in my place, then I owe you, God, my life and now I give it to you". — Then I popped into bed.

The next morning I discovered that something wonderful had happened to me, I had a great joy in my heart and I walked as though I had springs in my shoes. The Bible became a new book, or rather, I had new light on passages familiar to me, and would say to myself, "fancy not seeing that before". I longed for Sunday to come round so that I could go to church. Yes, for the first time in my life, I really wanted to go to church. The congregation left the singing to the choir, but I, who could not sing in tune, just had to sing at the top of my voice. It was springing up from inside me, just as Jesus told the woman at the well "---- the water that I shall give him shall be in him a well of water springing up into everlasting life". John 4:14.

My wife, who was more knowledgeable than me, remarked, "What has happened to you, have you been converted?" I replied that I did not know, but as I continued to read the Bible, I saw that this must be what had happened to me. "But as many as received Him, to them gave He power to become the sons of God, even to them that believe on His name:" John 1:12.

The church council meetings used to be very peaceful, but now I became a disturbing element, requiring, for example, that we do away with rented pews.

A colleague in the laboratories where I worked talked about the Baptist Church which he attended, causing me to go and see for myself that they had only a grand piano to accompany hearty singing. The pulpit was a rostrum holding several people and there was no choir, if I remember correctly.

I now had a thirst for more knowledge on how different denominations functioned, but I had such a sense of loyalty to the Church of England that I would not wander again, unless during a whole year all my suggestions at the church council meetings came to nought. They DID come to nought, and we moved house from Woolton to Huyton. My Baptist friend told me of a little mission church, a few miles from Huyton and belonging to the Liverpool City Mission. My wife was not yet converted and would go only to the Church of England. I, too, went to the Church of England a few times, then God made it clear to me that I was to seek out this little mission.

There were two small semi-detached cottages. One housed the missioner's family and the other had a meeting-room upstairs. There was a crooked notice-board which said, "We preach Christ crucified". And there was lank grass growing under the board. The doorway was dark and narrow. I said to myself, "Have I got to go in here?"

It was such a contrast to Woolton Parish Church, that it needed all my courage to enter and dash up the stairs. A bright-faced young man shook my hand, saying, "I was praying God would send somebody in". I knew I was that somebody!!

Over the window was a text "Ye must be Born Again". John 3:7. Below was a little platform. The congregation consisted mostly of teenagers, who were very keen Christians, fond of open-air meetings and of chorus singing. The leader was a very humble man, permitting others to do what they believed the Holy Ghost would have them to do. "Where the Spirit of the Lord is, there is liberty". 2 Cor. 3:17. I continued to attend regularly and I was amazed at what I was hearing: so much of it was new to me, but unquestionably biblical. They had different speakers each week; some were Liverpool City Missioners and some were missionaries on furlough. None were dressed in clerical clothes and none, I imagine, had degrees.

If we reflect on the sort of men that Jesus chose, we find that they are described as unlearned and ignorant men -- at least Peter and John were called such. Acts 4:13 says, "When they saw the boldness of Peter and John, and perceived that they were unlearned and ignorant men, they marvelled; and they took knowledge of them, that they had been with Jesus". Peter and John had just healed miraculously, a crippled man and Peter had preached faithfully, accusing the people of killing the Prince of Life and desiring the death of Jesus, rather than the death of a murderer.

Chapter 22 — CONVERSION OF MY WIFE EDITH

An evangelist associated with the "Young Life Campaign" was in Liverpool conducting a campaign in an undenominational church. Close friends of ours attended this church and invited us to come and hear the evangelist, Roy Hessian. Edith refused to go, because it was not in a Church of England. However, on the Sunday morning, Roy preached in an Anglican Church in South Kensington (Liverpool). The text was, "What meaneth then this bleating of the sheep —" 1 Sam. 15:14. Edith greatly enjoyed the sermon and, wanting to hear Roy preach again, was willing even to go to the undenominational church one evening. We went; Roy preached on "The Way of Salvation" and made an appeal for those wishing to accept Christ to come forward. Edith responded to the appeal, much to my surprise, although that was just what I had been praying for.

The next day, the devil kept whispering to me, "Your wife is not converted, your wife is not converted". It was so insistent that it was robbing me of my peace. So I hid myself behind a rack in the laboratory where I worked and prayed to God, asking Him to silence satan's voice, which He did!

When I arrived home from work and opened my front door, I heard singing, "Jesus gave her water that was not in the well". It was Edith singing as she was bathing the baby. She was not in the habit of singing choruses, and so I knew that this singing was confirmation of her conversion.

Yes, Jesus had given Edith the water that was not in the well. This water, of course, is the Holy Ghost (or Holy Spirit). Jesus speaks of this water that He would give as being "a well of water springing up into everlasting life". John 4:14.

Jesus exhorts us to keep His commandments, and so abide in His love, "even as I have kept my Father's commandments, and abide in His love". John 15:10. "These things have I spoken unto you, that my joy might remain in you, and that your joy might be full". John 15:11.

"If any man have not the Spirit of Christ, he is none of His". Rom. 8:9b. To be a christian, one not only has to have the right beliefs, but also one has to have the Spirit of Christ (the Holy Spirit) dwelling in him.

After her conversion, Edith attended this undenominational church regularly, because the minister gave good sound teaching sermons. On the Sunday evenings, she would now come with me to the little mission in the country. We had two little girls whom we took with us on our tandem bicycle; one child on the carrier and the other child on a saddle fastened to the horizontal crossbar, and we must have presented quite a picture as we made our way through the lanes, probably singing to the Lord, of joy and living water.

Chapter 23 — A GOSPEL WEEKEND

The little mission in the country started to "Come Alive". Often tears would come to my eyes. Conversions were frequent and the little upper room was getting full. People did not want to go home after the Sunday evening service, and sometimes it would be 10 p.m. before they all left. The Monday evening prayer meeting was well attended and it may well be that this was a great source of power.

A big proportion of the congregation were teenagers who had so surrendered themselves to the Lord, that there was no doubt whatever but that Jesus had first place in their lives, in their interests and in their time. There would be at least one, and sometimes two, open-air meetings a week. The Bible says, "But seek ye first the kingdom of God, and His righteousness; and all these things shall be added unto you". Matt. 6:33. In the open air, it was not prearranged who would do the speaking, but, on the contrary, it was always open for anyone in the circle to speak, sing, testify or whatever, as they felt the Lord leading them. Our leader was such a humble man that the Holy Ghost could do the leading. I used to stand with them in the circle wishing that I had the ability to preach like the others. But one day I felt the Lord saying to me, "If somebody asked you the way to the railway station, could you direct them?" I said, "Yes, Lord, easily". It seemed as though the Lord asked me, "Can you not tell the people how you became born-again, — converted?" Yes, I could and I did. So began my speaking for Jesus and I would like to encourage others to do likewise.

We were a very united little band and one day, when somebody said, "Let us have a gospel weekend", we all said yes and started to plan the programme. Some of us were working on the Saturday morning, so we planned to start with a midday meal in our garden, to be followed by some open-air meetings, one after another, in various parts of Huyton, including the outside of the cinema. Then we were to drop a "gospel bomb" on a public house close to the little mission in Tarbok. This was to be followed by an all-night prayer meeting in the mission.

The weather looked bad that Saturday morning with dark clouds, but not a spot of rain fell. We had a good hearing at our many open-air meetings, and at the cinema there was a queue of people waiting to go in, and we felt challenged to preach our hardest to hold the people's attention. Next, two of us went to the posh nearby public house to distribute tracts. We asked permission to do this from an attendant at the bar. We approached with fear and trembling, but to my surprise the attendant said, "Certainly, this is a dreadful place". I have described it as "posh", but evidently it was posh only in outside appearance.

Next, we went to Tarbok to drop our "gospel bomb" on the pub, near the mission. The pub had a convenient forecourt for us to have an open-air meeting. We started to sing, as our custom was, to the accompaniment of a piano accordian, but there was so much noise going on inside the pub, that it seemed doubtful if we could be heard. So I went inside to make sure, and came out saying, "It's of no use, we cannot be heard and we shall have to wait until the patrons come out". But I was wrong, for immediately some young men came out, saying that we were disturbing their singing, and they told us to clear off, and that there was no need for us to be there, as they would all be at communion the next day! It was then obvious to us that we could be heard, and that we should continue with our witness, which we did. As closing time was approaching we felt led by the Lord to be even more aggressive. So we formed ourselves into two lines, one on either side of the doorway, so that the patrons leaving the pub would need to pass between our two lines and be subject to our witness.

We had been joined by some keen Christians from Liverpool, who had heard of our planned Gospel "bomb", and all-night prayer meeting. A fine-looking young woman stood on the pub steps witnessing, and a young man from the pub raised a beer bottle over her head in a threatening way. She saw the threat but took no notice. I was about two yards away and I became aware that this woman could not be harmed because either the Lord Jesus or an angel was there protecting her. This awareness of the divine protection had a terrific effect on me.

The next thing to happen was for one of the patrons to bring his motor cycle up between our two lines and to rev his engine to drown our witness. He stopped opposite me, and I found that, by putting my mouth close to his ear, I had no difficulty telling him who Jesus was and why He died, and what he had to do about it. I then prayed that God would stop the engine, which He did immediately, and the bike had to be removed.

Another young man, seeing what had happened, brought his motor bike into the same spot and began revving the engine. I spoke in his ear, as I had done in his companion's ear, and I prayed that God would stop the engine, which He did, and the second had to be removed in defeat. The remainder of the patrons passed between our lines, and were subject to "Gospel shots", (quotations from scripture) etc.: I would have expected that they would have lost no time in getting into their cars and driving off as quickly as possible, but on the contrary there were several little groups forming, each with one of our members talking to pub patrons about Jesus. This went on for quite a while, nobody seemed in a hurry to depart. I talked to a woman who had brought her daughter to the pub and who both were once members of the Salvation Army.

When at last we could get away we went into the Mission for an all-night prayer meeting. We sang and prayed all night, nobody prayed more than once, and all our singing was without the use of hymn books. There were no pauses, and very soon, so it seemed, it was morning. The stars were shining brightly, and so were we. Only one of our members felt any sleepiness whatever.

The following Saturday evening two of us went again to the pub, to see the effect of our "bomb". There was only about half the number of cars there than the week before. Whilst we were making our assessment the two young men who had tried to drown our witness by revving their motor-bike engines, came up to us and thanked us for the tracts we had given them, saying that they had read them when they had got home.

You may think, dear reader, that it was rather improper for us to have taken such aggressive steps. All I can say in reply is that the Lord seemed to be leading us, and certainly He seemed to be with us because of the miracles that He performed. The sense of His protective presence when the young woman was threatened; His stopping of both the motor-bike engines, and the appreciation of so many who stopped by to hear the Gospel, rather than jump into their cars in disgust.

It may be remembered that the patrons of the pub told us that they would be at communion the next morning, and that there was no need for us to be there witnessing to them. We, of course, thought otherwise. Manifestly, a lot of trouble results from drinking alcohol, and it is relevant to search the scriptures on the subject. Paul advises Timothy to take a LITTLE wine for his stomach's sake, (1 Tim. 5:23). We read of Jesus turning water into wine at the wedding feast in Cana, (John 2:1—10). Thus it might seem, at first, that the Bible has nothing to say against drinking wine, but such is not the case. Proverbs 20 verse 1, says, "Wine is a mocker, strong drink is raging: and whosoever is deceived thereby is not wise". In Eph. 5:18 we read "And be not drunk with wine, wherein is excess; but be filled with the Spirit". A bishop (an elder) must not be given to wine (1 Tim. 3:3 & Titus 1:7). Aged women should not be given to much wine (Titus 2:3). Noah made himself drunk with wine and became uncovered, (Gen. 9:21). In Exodus 29:40 & Leviticus 23:13 & Num. 15:5, we read of wine being employed for drink offerings. But in Numbers 6:3 we read of men and women separating themselves unto the Lord, taking the vow of a Nazarite, "shall separate themselves from wine and strong drink". Samson was chosen to begin to deliver Israel out of the hand of the Philistines, and he was to be a Nazarite (abstaining from strong drink) Judges 13:5. Similarly, John the Baptist, who was to be great in the sight of the Lord, and to turn many of the children of Israel to the Lord their God, "and shall drink neither wine nor strong drink; and he shall be filled with the Holy Ghost, even from his mother's womb". (Luke 1:15, 16). Also deacons must not be given to much wine, (1 Tim. 3:8). Samson's mother was not allowed, by an angel, to drink wine or strong drink, (Judges 13:4 & 14). Samuel's mother, Hannah, had not drunk wine nor strong drink when praying for a son to lend to the Lord, as long as he liveth, (1 Sam. 1:15). Samuel's mother vowed that if the Lord of hosts would give her "a male child, then I will give him unto the Lord all the days of his life, and there shall no razor come upon his head". (1 Sam. 1:11). The uncut hair indicates a Nazarite vow, which would include abstinence from wine and strong drink.

In the New Testament, we have also "and be not drunk with wine, in which is excess; but be filled with the Spirit", (Eph. 5:18). Drunkenness is clearly a bar to inheriting the kingdom of God, (1 Cor. 6:10 & Gal. 5:21). The church in all its denominations, should be teaching all this. Romans 12:2 says, "and be not conformed to this world: but be ye transformed by the renewing of your mind, that ye may prove what is that good, and acceptable, and perfect, will of God". James 4:4 tells us "that the friendship of the world is enmity with God". "If any man love the world, the love of the Father is not in him", (1 John 2:15).

Chapter 24 — FAITHFUL WITNESSING — AND THE DEVIL'S ATTACKS

One of the mission's young men worked in a brick works. He was a very keen Christian and witnessed faithfully to his workmates. However they did not appreciate the young man's efforts to win them for the Lord, so they went to their boss demanding that the young man — I think his name was Victor — be dismissed; otherwise they would go on strike. The boss was quite unwilling to dismiss Victor, but Victor was quite willing to be dismissed. So Victor was sacked, and in a matter of a few days he was offered employment by a Christian employer, with his wages fixed 50% higher than what he had been receiving from the brickyard.

I think it was this same Victor who had to appear before a judge at the beginning of the Second World War, because he was a conscientious objector. His chief concern was that he should make a good confession of Christ before the court, rather than that he should be exempt from military service. At the start of the hearing he told the judge that he was a Christian and that if he were exempted from military service he would ask permission to sing a verse of a hymn in court. The judge replied that he would see about that later.

The judge could find no fault in Victor and let him off completely from military service, saying, "The army has lost a valiant soldier". He gave Victor permission to sing his verse of a hymn. Victor sang his verse and a newspaper report of the trial said, "The court was visibly affected". Jesus said, "When they bring you unto the synagogues, and unto magistrates, and powers, take ye no thought how or what thing ye shall answer, or what ye shall say: for the Holy Ghost shall teach you in the same hour what you ought to say". Luke 12:11—12.

The war having started, some of the members of the mission were convinced that we no longer would be allowed to have our usual open-air meetings. When they were asked why not, there

58

didn't seem to be any really concrete reason given for their conviction on the matter. Consequently, I became suspicious that the father of lies had been busy. Who is the father of lies? The devil: (John 8:44). It is one of the devil's strategies to deceive people, to get them to believe in a lie. He told Eve, "Ye shall not surely die" — in direct contradiction of what God had said. So I decided I would test the matter by going to the police station, and I was told that we could still have our open-air meetings.

On another occasion, when we were on a preaching tour in Wales and were standing in a wide main street, the suggestion that we should have an open-air meeting was met with the response that we would not be allowed to have one there. To the question — why not? — there seemed to be no satisfactory answer, so a trip was made to the police station. We were given permission without hesitation and, additionally, we were told that if we went into a certain street, we would find a queue of people waiting for a bus, and we would have a captive audience. It would seem that once again the devil was trying to scare us with lies.

Is it not true that too little attention has been given to the ways of the devil? and hence we are not very well equipped to meet his attacks. In Acts 10:38 we read, "God anointed Jesus of Nazareth with the Holy Ghost and with power: who went about doing good, and healing all that were oppressed of the devil; for God was with Him". Oppressed of the devil and needing healing! — many may be in that condition today without anybody realising it. In Luke 13:11 we read about "a woman who had a spirit of infirmity eighteen years, and was bowed together, and could in no wise lift up herself". Jesus laid his hands on her; and immediately she was made straight and glorified God. In verse 16, Jesus tells us that it was satan who had bound this woman. In 1 John 3:8b we read, "For this purpose the Son of God was manifested, that He might destroy the works of the devil".

Why are we told to put on the whole armour of God? — Eph. 6:11. It is so that ye may be able to stand against the wiles of the devil. It was the devil that put it into Judas Iscariot's heart to betray Jesus, Jn. 13:2. In modern times we read in our newspapers of happenings so cruel, and so unnatural, that it would seem that the devil is behind them, or at least behind some of them.

In the parable of the sower we are warned that the devil "taketh away the word (of God) out of their (the hearers) hearts, lest they should believe and be saved". Luke 8:12. It would appear, then, that the devil has been busy in the church stealing away the word of God, robbing many of any knowledge of the way of salvation, and the fact that Jesus is coming back, and the fact that miracles are happening today.

We make a big mistake if we underestimate the extent of the devil's activity and the devil's power. About one-third of the healings Jesus performed, were needed because of the devil's activity. The power of the devil is indicated by his statement that he would give to Jesus "all the kingdoms of the world, and the glory of them", if Jesus would fall down and worship him. Matt. 4:8 & 9. Nevertheless, we know that Jesus gave his disciples power and authority over all devils, (Luke 9:1). And in Luke 10:17 we read, "and the seventy returned again with joy, saying, Lord, even the devils are subject unto us through Thy name".

I, personally, have heard, on two occasions, a woman scream out loudly during an indoor meeting, due presumably to the devil, and reminding me of the boy in scripture who needed deliverance. He suddenly cried out, Luke 9:39. The disciples were not able to do what was required, and when Jesus commanded the foul spirit to come out of the boy, he (the spirit) cried out, Mark 9:26.

Chapter 25 — A PREACHING TOUR IN WALES

A party of about half a dozen of us set out to preach the Gospel in Wales during an Easter weekend. We had a small car and a trailer to carry our luggage and food, and some of us were on bicycles. I was in charge of the catering and I was very inexperienced in matters of the Spirit. It was a grand opportunity for me to acquire some first-hand knowledge! Our first stop was in Warrington for an open-air meeting. I held up a banner, feeling alas, a little ashamed of what I was doing! There did not seem to be much power in that meeting. Our next stop was in Mold, I think. Here we fixed up sleeping accommodation in a disused Salvation Army room. We preached at a bus-stop, as mentioned in the previous chapter. Our sleeping quarters were dirty and dusty, and the floor was hard to sleep upon. The Bible says, "Endure hardness, as a good soldier of Jesus Christ". 2 Tim. 2:3.

The next morning, Friday, we preached at a crossroads where there were traffic lights. When the lights turned red we had a captive audience for a few minutes. One vehicle was a laundry van with two boys on the back. The boys heard us, and we were to meet them again later in another town. With the object of finding an opportunity for an indoor meeting we called on the vicar. He had just returned home after taking a three-hour service. He was tired out and looked very dejected and he told us that he still had the evening service to take. We said we would take it for him, but he told us that he could not accept our offer, as he would need to obtain his bishop's permission for that. He looked so forlorn, and we, in contrast, were so young and full of life that the situation seemed ridiculous and nonsensical. I wonder what Jesus thought? So many of us, when we set out to serve God, end up by being slaves to mere man!

Next, we called on the Methodist minister. He had a concert

arranged for the evening, but he was willing for us to speak after the concert. This we did, and we seemed to have a good hearing, with most of the people staying on after the concert in order to hear us.

The following Saturday, we set off for Ruthin. Here we were kindly given sleeping accommodation, in a room belonging to the Presbyterian Church. We marched all over Ruthin singing choruses to the accompaniment of a piano accordian. One of our favourites was "There is power, power, wonder-working power, In the blood of the Lamb!" The little band knew lots of choruses off by heart and loved singing them. Personally, I was of little help, since I had but little voice, could not sing in tune, and knew very few choruses. The 'posh' churches with which I was acquainted were too posh to sing choruses.

On Sunday afternoon during a time of private prayer and preparation for an open-air meeting in the evening, I had an impression that God was going to use one of our lads who was so lacking in eloquence that in ordinary conversation, it was difficult to make out what he was trying to say. Had our group been under normal leadership, it would be most unlikely that the lad would have been called upon to speak. I've already mentioned that our leader was a very humble man — so humble, in fact that he did not call on anybody to speak or not to speak, but he left that to the Holy Ghost. Consequently, the Holy Ghost was given elbow room to choose "whom he will, when he will". This is perhaps one of the greatest shocks you will meet as you continue to read.

This great shock is, that the Holy Ghost will lead, if we will let Him, and that He will use people that, humanly speaking, are unsuitable. I believe it was the Holy Ghost that led me to pray for this lad that afternoon. I said nothing to him, nor to anybody else about the matter, but got on with preparing a meal, which was my job. However, nobody wanted to eat; God had taken our appetites away! After attending the Presbyterian Church in the evening, we went into the market square for a planned open-air meeting. The weather changed, in that the cold wind dropped; I took off my thick overcoat, feeling that God was with us. We began to sing choruses, and people began to gather round us. People in the nearby hotel came to the windows, and to the door, to see what all the noise was about, and they were still there two hours later!

The lad I had prayed for stepped into the centre of the circle and began to preach. God not only gave him a message to preach, but also perfectly clear English in which to deliver it. Another lad, who could not normally speak in public because he stammered badly, stepped into the ring and spoke for several minutes without stammering.

So **Shock No.12:** That God is still choosing speakers who, humanly speaking, are quite unsuitable, and having chosen them, He performs miracles enabling them to do the impossible; some christians have believed and taught that miracles ceased in the first century!

We have already mentioned, in chapter 19, that "God hath chosen the weak things of the world to confound the things which are mighty; and base things of the world, and things which are despised, hath God chosen, yea, and things which are not, to bring to nought things that are: that no flesh should glory in His presence", 1 Cor. 1:27—29.

We had a good hearing, and the two boys in the laundry van who heard us in Mold, now accepted Christ as their Saviour, and they came to the place where we were staying, to have the scriptures opened up to them; and they were back again, early the next morning, for some more teaching.

The man at the hotel door offered to give us a cheque. We refused it because we were fussy about money, and would have nothing to do with taking money from the unsaved. Paul in 1 Cor. 9:14 makes it clear that they which preach the gospel may live off the gospel, but nevertheless in verse 12 he tells us that he did not make use of that 'power', lest he should hinder the gospel. It was 10 p.m. before we stopped this open-air meeting, which had lasted two hours. The appetites of our party returned to them and we enjoyed the meal we had refused earlier.

The next day two of us thought it would be proper for us to call on the vicar, before leaving Ruthin for home. We found that he was in the church about to commence a service. He invited us to join in. We knelt down near the front of the church and I remember very clearly praying silently, saying "Lord, I don't know what to pray, but do whatever is Your will", (or words similar to that). The vicar was intoning the service, but he seemed to be finding it difficult because he kept breaking into ordinary speech!

On the way back to Liverpool, we came to a village green near Queensferry. Here we decided to stop and have an open-air meeting. I had no intention of speaking, I had nothing prepared and my throat was sore from the very small amount of speaking I had done; also my voice was hoarse. Nevertheless, I found myself preaching with a clear voice and no sore throat, a message given to me suddenly, without effort. It was the first time it had happened to me and it was a wonderful experience. I wondered if that was how John Wesley did some of his open-air preaching. When we arrived back at the mission in the evening, we found that our dear sisters in Christ had prepared a 'welcome home' meal for us, and they were keen to hear how the Lord had dealt with us.

I would like to summarise the miracles of this trip:—
1.   The loss of appetite before the Sunday evening's work. We had not planned a fast, and we didn't intend to fast, but evidently God thought it necessary, and so He took away our appetites.
2.   The weather suddenly changed during the evening. The cold wind suddenly dropped, just as we were about to start our open-air meeting. I was able to take off my thick overcoat, knowing Who had stopped the cold wind.
3.   The gathering of quite a crowd in the market square to hear us. We learned later, that the market square is normally deserted on a Sunday evening.
4.   The rapt attention of the crowd, including those at the door and windows of the hotel, for the whole of the meeting lasting two hours, despite the fact that there was no quality in us. No preaching ability worth mentioning; none of us had been to a Bible college; none of us was an orator, none of us was a minister, etc. No, God drew the crowd and He held them, miraculously.
5.   The chief speaker was given speaking ability that, obviously, was a miracle.
6.   A stammerer lost his stammer for just long enough to preach.
7.   Two boys accepted Christ; they became converted.
8.   I was able to preach on a village green, when I had no intention of speaking, because, (a) I was only an amateur, (b) I had almost lost my voice and my throat was sore, and (c) I had nothing prepared. But God swept these disabilities away.

I have taken the liberty of repeating what has already been written because it seemed so important that we should grasp the fact that our God is a God of miracles today, as in all the thousands of years preceding today. In Mark 16:20 we read, "And they went forth, and preached everywhere". Note, not just in their meeting-rooms and chapels. It goes on to say, "the Lord working with them, and confirming the word with signs following". Matt. 28:20 says, "and lo, I am with you alway, even unto the end of the world".

Why am I emphasising the importance of miracles? In Acts 9:32—35 we read of two whole towns, Lydda and Saron, turning to the Lord when they saw Aeneas, who had suddenly been healed by God working through Peter. Aeneas had been in bed for eight years with paralysis, and was cured immediately by Peter saying to him,

"Jesus Christ maketh thee whole: arise, and make thy bed". In 1 Cor. 4:20 we read, "For the kingdom of God is not in word, but in power". Is it not our custom, generally, to put the emphasis on 'eloquence' rather than power, when training people for the ministry?

We might well ask, "Why was it that Peter was used to work such mighty miracles, when his background was so lowly?" We are warned in 1 Cor. 3:20 that the Lord knoweth the thoughts of the wise, that they are in vain.

It would seem that the Lord's work cannot be done by human wisdom, that it takes what only God can give. If you, dear reader, hold the theory that miracles ended with the first century, please read some of the modern books which record much greater miracles than I have witnessed during this trip to Wales! But be warned, satan will do his best to keep you from being influenced by reading such books. You may be in fellowship with Christians who have a strong tradition of belief that miracles ended in the first century. If so, it will not be easy for you to accept the reverse contention. In Matt. 15:6 we read, "Thus have ye made the commandment of God of none effect by your tradition".

Most of us put so much confidence in the tradition of our own denomination, that it becomes difficult for us to accept truth contrary to our denomination. There is always a danger of us putting our tradition on a higher place than the word of God, the Bible. There is also danger of us glorifying in men. 1 Cor. 3:21 says, "Therefore let no man glory in men", and the reason is that even the thoughts of the wise are vain, which was stated in the previous verse, verse 20.

I ought to define what I mean by a miracle. I mean a supernatural event, and not just one of the 'wonders' of nature, like the birth of a baby, or a chrysalis turning into a butterfly.

If you have an open mind and desire to go forward in the things of Christ, "unto a perfect man, unto the measure of the stature of the fullness of Christ", Ephs. 4:13b, then doubtless God will bring to your notice books which will help you! Jeremiah 33:3 says, "Call unto me, and I will answer thee, and show thee great and mighty things, which thou knowest not".

E

Chapter 26 — GOOD AND BAD

The little mission in the country increased in numbers, and the folks had to sit on the stairs, because the upper room became full and overflowing. Conversions were almost a weekly occurrence. On one evening the preacher was a young man who gave such a poor sermon, that I thought no-one could possibly be saved through it. But, nevertheless, someone was saved that evening!

One week night, when normally there was no meeting, I went along to collect a whitewash brush that I had been using there. As several other people turned up, under the impression that there was to be a meeting, our leader suggested that we had better have a meeting, since there was quite a number of us present. Several people spoke and each time the word given was against smoking. We learnt later, that one of the young men present was trying to give up smoking. Obviously, God had arranged everything! Each speaker had said he did not know why he was speaking about smoking.

Now, it is my painful duty to relate to you some bad things. The Bible does not shun to relate bad things. Whilst it brings out David's high qualities, it also records his sin. In the New Testament, Jesus says to Peter, "Get thee behind me, Satan: thou art an offense unto me: for thou savourest not the things that be of God, but those that be of men". Matt. 16:23.

Murmuring started amongst us; not against one another, but against the Liverpool City Mission, of which we were a part. Some thought that we should not be a part of the L. C. Mission. Actually, the organisation left us to pursue our own ways and never, so far as I knew, hindered us in any way, but rather the reverse. There did not seem to be any reason for the murmuring, so I suspect that it was satan trying to destroy us. Whilst we were well up in the knowledge of scriptures associated with salvation, we

66

were not well up in a knowledge of scriptures associated with behaviour or anything else. So it was easy for satan to get in and cause disunity, where previously there had been none.

Sadly, the murmuring grew to the point where a number met to talk over what they were going to do. No conclusion was reached so far as I know, but alas we seemed to have grieved the Holy Ghost, for conversions stopped happening and our numbers decreased. Our Lord, in his prayer to his Father, prayed, "Holy Father, keep through thine own name those whom thou hast given me, that they may be one, as we are". John 17:11b. In 1 Cor. 1:10b, we are all told to, "speak the same thing, and that there be no divisions among you". Most Christians know that there should be real unity, but there does not, yet, seem to be an adequate effort being put in to achieve it. Most of us love our separate 'denominations' and are convinced that our denomination is better than the others. It is time, is it not, for us to be more humble and more willing to hear those who have beliefs differing from our own. It is time for us to question the rightness of our traditions, especially where they do differ from other traditions.

In the realm of christian behaviour there is alas, amazing ignorance of what the scriptures teach and one hears, sometimes, of actions that could not be further from scripture. God is very 'fussy' about our behaviour, and about our attitudes towards one another. In one place He says, "for if ye forgive men their trespasses, your heavenly Father will also forgive you: but if ye forgive not men their trespasses, neither will your Father forgive your trespasses". Matt. 6:14 & 15.

Then there is the matter of not exercising lordship and kingly authority over our brothers and sisters in Christ, Luke 22:25—26. What a difference it would make in the church if we all acted on that instruction! 1 Peter 5:3.

Much could be said about behaviour being not what it should be, but it will suffice if I call your attention to the behaviour of the two leading denominations in Northern Ireland, where there seems to be more hatred than love.

Chapter 27 — TEARS OF JOY

The Old Testament teaches very clearly that adherence to God's word brings blessings and disobedience brings curses. Deuteronomy, chapter 28 gives us quite a list of the blessings and quite a list of the curses.

In the New Testament, God deals with his people a little differently in that the blessings and curses seem to be rather more spiritual than material; and God shows great patience with the sinner "not willing that any should perish". 2 Pet. 3:9. Nevertheless, I can testify to material blessings, just as many others can and do . . . . .

I had been very happy working in the laboratories of a large electrical engineering firm and I imagined that I would spend the remainder of my working days that way. But when the war broke out, I got unsettled for various reasons, and one day I decided I would leave the industry. I would have liked to have had an engineering business of my own, but with the war being on, it seemed very unlikely that I would be allowed materials, as they were required for the war effort.

It seemed that the best thing for me to do was to start farming. My wife and I had already made the decision to go farming, when we suddenly realised that we had not sought the Lord's will on the matter. So we repented of that, and that same evening, in our scripture reading, we were given scriptures clearly indicating that we would prosper in farming.

The scriptures were not selected by us, but were part of the normal sequence of our reading. They were so applicable to our situation that I had them printed on cards, which I distributed to my friends. Looking back, I believe I was in error, and that although I had received God's permission and promise of protection, it did not necessarily mean that that was the path He would have chosen for me. No. I think He was leaving me to go my own way — just as parents sometimes have to let their children go their own way. There is a hymn that goes:—

"Have Thine own way, Lord,   Mould me and make me
Have Thine own way;   After Thy will,
Thou art the Potter,   While I am waiting
I am the clay.   Yielded and still".

I knew nothing whatever about farming. I had kept a few hens and had a dog!! So I would be starting from scratch. I took a correspondence course which was very helpful, and I started to collect all my bits and pieces together ready for a move. I had only £600 as capital, which even in those days, 1941, was a very small amount indeed for stocking a farm. It was obvious that I could not both buy a farm and stock it; I needed to rent a farm. Farms to let were scarce, and they usually went to the owner's friends or relatives.

A farm agent in Exeter, when he learned of my lack of experience, told me that I stood no chance whatever of obtaining a farm to let, because no owner would let a farm to a novice. Also that I stood no chance whatever of making ends meet, financially. He said to me, "Go home and forget about it". He was an elderly man and, obviously, he knew what he was talking about. But I knew that I would get a farm, because of the scriptures which came to me on the evening we decided to go farming.

Sometime later, I was back again in the same agent's office. The elderly man was away, but his assistant was there, so I said, "Have you a farm to let?" He replied, "Haven't we seen you here before?" I said, "Yes, but have you any farms to let?" His reply was, "Well, as a matter of fact, we have one farm, but it is not a fat farm". He let me have the particulars. The farm, named "Nethercot", was situated on the edge of Dartmoor. The owner was not a farmer, he had bought the land, 93 acres, for £600, added a little modern house and shippon (cow shed), hoping to sell the whole for profit. He was willing to have me as a tenant.

My dear wife was brought up in a London suburb; she had never lived 'rough', under primitive conditions, and many small farmhouses that I had viewed were lacking modern conveniences, and were decidedly rough. Devon was her favourite county, however. When I told her that I had secured a farm and that it was in Devon, and that it had a little modern house with a bathroom, I burst into tears at the goodness of God. Not only had He provided me, an amateur, with a rented farm, but He had, as well, provided

Nethercot Farm — 1941

one with a modern house for my wife, and one in her own favourite county. Philip. 4:19 says, "My God shall supply all your need according to His riches in glory by Christ Jesus". Rom. 8:28 says, "And we know that all things work together for good to them that love God, to them who are the called according to His purpose".

My bits and pieces were too many for one moving-van, so instead of hiring a second van at a cost of £25, I bought a good car for £12 and a trailer for £16. We packed the overflow of goods on the trailer and onto the roof of the car, so for £28, only £3 extra, I had made a useful addition to my possessions.

Cars were very cheap in 1941, due to the war with Germany, and as we travelled along to Devon, folks thought that we had been bombed out of our home. Our route seemed to lie parallel with that of the German airplanes droning away overhead. Road signs had been removed and we were not allowed to use headlights, however we arrived safely in the dark, and set about settling ourselves in . . . . . all so very exciting and very adventurous!!

The next day we needed milk; this I expected to be able to buy at a neighbouring farm quite readily, but it was not so easy as that for they did not have a retail licence. The nearest shop was in Okehampton 3 miles away, so we had to make do with skimmed milk for a short time. We also needed potatoes, which should not have been any problem, since I had bought about five sacks of them, which were still on the farm. So along I went with car and trailer to collect them from the place where they had been dumped. But alas, I was not strong enough to lift a sack full of potatoes, I could only roll one sack over another until at last one sack dropped into the trailer. A year or so later, I could lift a 1¼ cwt. sack of feeding cake, carry it on my back and load it into my car, without difficulty. My strength seemed almost to have doubled.

A kind neighbouring farmer suggested that I should buy a 100 day-old chicks and that he would lend me his apparatus for rearing them. I had never reared any chicks before, but by following his instructions I reared about 97 out of the 100. Edith was given some duck eggs and she reared, I think, the whole number.

There were on the farm a large number of poultry folding units, the property of my landlord. These needed dismantling and loading onto a lorry. I gave my landlord an estimate of the cost for doing this, which was accepted. As I set about undoing the nuts and bolts — an apparently menial job — I was very happy. I was basking in the freedom of being my own master; also enjoying the fresh open air. A little bit of engineering skill was involved because the nuts had rusted on to the bolts.

By taking into my employment a man who had been a farmer, I had — what I needed badly — a skilled farm worker to lean on! My neighbours were wonderfully kind and seemed to be almost as interested in my welfare as in their own. One day I heard the rumble of horses and carts on the road in front of my house, and I wondered where they were going to. They turned into my farm! They had come to cart my hay in, and they had acted on their own initiative, knowing that the hay was ready for stacking. I found the mutual help that went on between the farmers very pleasing. Does not the Bible say, "love thy neighbour as thyself", Matt. 19:19b? Everything, or almost everything, went so well that it was quite obvious to me that the farm was being run by God. After my second season, I had a rick of corn, which was so good, that it was described as the best in the district.

But I want to tell you about the exception to things going well. I needed a tractor, and bought one second-hand, and since this was something I could handle, being an engineer, it was as though God had left me to handle it! My field of oats was ready for cutting, but very soon I was unable to start the tractor. The trouble proved to be a crack in one of the cylinders. This allowed the cooling water to get into the other cylinders, so preventing them from firing. The supplier was an honest man. He knew there was a crack, but he thought he had repaired it successfully. He exchanged that tractor for another one, which was larger and initially more costly, although I don't think I had to pay any more for it. All went well for a time. The oil level in the sump was checkable by means of two cocks, one above the other. When these cocks were opened momentarily, oil should run out of the lower cock, but not out of the higher one. These cocks had left-hand threads, and one day I forgot about the left-hand thread and consequently, when I thought I had fully closed it, I had actually left a cock fully open. I ran the tractor and siezed up a big-end!

Things I knew nothing about went well, but things that I thought I could manage went wrong! There is a lesson here. So often in life, things that we run go wrong. "All we like sheep have gone astray; we have turned every one to his own way; --" Isaiah 53:6. Apparently, to go our own way is to go astray! We always need our Heavenly Shepherd to guide us. I was now just about to make a very big mistake!

I fully realised that my farm was a miraculous gift from God (lucky fellow), and I also realised that God was helping me to run it (lucky fellow), but I considered myself quite free to make my own decisions. It was my farm! When I fully understood the meaning of the description given to me by the agent that "it is not a fat farm" — meaning that the land does not produce heavy crops, then I reasoned that it was silly to farm on poor land. Without consulting God, who had given me the farm, I gave in my notice to my landlord to terminate the lease, at the end of the agreed three-year period. To me, it was just a matter of common sense, of sound business sense! A farmer friend told me that no experienced farmer would expect to make a profit, on my farm, in under four years. So what was wrong with that decision to move? Quite a lot!; but I must give you a little detail, before I can make the error clear.

Right from the start, I was not conscious of losing money. There were a lot of wild rabbits on the farm and catching and selling these provided a substantial income. Then eggs from about fifty laying hens helped a little, until I was able to buy some cows and sell the milk. Also I had some neighbours' sheep grazing on my fields and paying me money for the privilege. But what was important was that I went in heavily for ploughing the old grassland, reseeding it with more productive grass and grazing it off with sheep. This raised the fertility of the land considerably and thus reasonably heavy crops could now be obtained.

On the christian witness side; Edith and I had started a Sunday school in a little nearby chapel, and that had drawn in almost every child in the district. Everything was going well, so why did I want to move? There is only one answer, to make more money! What's wrong with that? One needs enough money to live! Yes, true; but the Bible has some surprising things to say about money! "But they that will be rich fall into temptation and a snare, and into many foolish and hurtful lusts, which drown men in destruction and

perdition". 1 Tim. 6:9. We have heard of many rich 'pop' stars
falling into foolish and hurtful lusts and even destroying their lives.
The next verse says, "-- the love of money is the root of all evil:
which while some coveted after, they have erred from the faith, and
pierced themselves through with many sorrows", 1 Tim. 6:10. In
another place the scripture says, "-- ye rich men, weep and howl for
your miseries that shall come upon you ---", James 5, 1—6. The
context here shows that the reference is to riches gained by
oppression, by wrong means.

So, what was wrong then in my looking for a better farm?
Complete failure to realize why I am in the world! and so, getting
my priorities wrong. Why did God make man? and Stanley in
particular? Obviously for God's pleasure, and equally obviously,
none of us remain in the world very long. So, was Stanley put in the
world primarily just to keep himself, and others, alive and happy
and nothing more than that? What about after death? The Bible
says of a certain farmer who had so much goods, and who said to
his soul -- 'take thine ease, eat, drink, and be merry' -- "Thou fool,
this night thy soul shall be required of thee: then whose shall those
things be, which thou hast provided? So is he that layeth up
treasure for himself, and is not rich toward God". Luke 12:
16—21. Another scripture says, "Lay up for yourselves treasures in
heaven, where neither moth nor rust doth corrupt, and where
thieves do not break through nor steal; For where your treasure is,
there will your heart be also". Matt. 6:20, 21.

What are treasures in heaven? One obvious treasure is a very
close association with no less a person than Jesus Christ Himself.
This is so close an association that it is likened to marriage! —
Revn. 19:7. "Blessed are they which are called unto the marriage
supper of the Lamb. And he saith unto me, These are the true
sayings of God". Revn. 19:9. We are to make ourselves ready for
this marriage, see Revn. 19:7. Another treasure in heaven is,
obviously, people whom we have helped to get in to heaven. The
gathering in of those people for heaven is likened to the gathering
in of the farmer's harvest. The Bible says that for this kind of
harvest the labourers are few and that we should pray the Lord of
the harvest, "that he will send forth labourers into his harvest".
Matt. 9:37, 38. What other treasures are there in heaven?
Everlasting life, John 3:16. Freedom from sorrow and crying and
pain, all things having been made new. Revn. 21:4, 5. Also, God
himself dwelling with them. Revn. 21:3.

It would seem then, that our purpose for being in the world is
primarily that we might gain, or lose, a much better world with
God and everlasting life. Whether or not we gain much wealth here

is important only in so far as wealth may hinder our access to everlasting life! Matt. 19:24. Jesus did not seek material wealth, for he said, "the Son of man hath not where to lay his head". Matt. 8:20. In Acts 3:6, Peter said, "Silver and gold have I none --". So, on reflection, my priority was wrong, in that I was seeking material things as a first priority. The Bible says, "Seek ye first the kingdom of God, and His righteousness; and all these things shall be added unto you". Matt. 6:33. I was attending to the normal christian activities of Bible reading, prayer and attendance at a place of worship on Sundays, and witnessing to my fellow beings.

The Sunday school was going along very well. Edith, being a trained teacher was, of course, the one to take the leading part, but there was also another christian lady farmer close by, who also helped. On Sunday school anniversary day, the children were taught special things to do. I can't remember in detail what they were, but I know they definitely were Bible-based things and not just entertainment. I think one item was 'A Gospel Train'. An official minister, who had come out from Okehampton to speak at this service remarked afterwards that he was both surprised and pleased that we had stuck to the Bible. It had not even occurred to us to do otherwise! My younger daughter, Dawn, who was then quite young, sang, "Bye and bye, we'll see the King". (I think she paused in the middle of it to say to her sister Jillian, "Jill, don't look at me!", and it has stayed in my mind ever since.)

Some years later, when Edith and I paid a visit to this area, we heard that several of the children, now well into their teens, had given their hearts to the Lord whilst they were in Sunday school. One, I think, was training to be a nurse in a hospital near Torquay. Another had been baptised and was going on well with the Lord. It gave us much pleasure to hear this welcome news! Oh yes, we have some treasure in heaven! and won't we be glad when we meet all those that we knew here on earth! But we need to remember that the Bible says that only a few find their way there, despite our imagination to the contrary. It says in Matt. 7:14, "-- strait is the gate, and narrow is the way, which leadeth unto life, and few there be that find it". Also, in Matt. 20:16, it says, "-- for many are called, but few chosen".

Returning to the farm, my farm worker was fond of horses and I left him to choose a horse that he liked. He chose a highly-spirited young mare, I think about 3 years old, who was something approaching a race horse. She was called 'Beauty'. One of her tasks was to pull my trailer up a steep hill, after it was loaded with churns of milk, and myself. This was a daily routine for taking the milk to a collecting point at the top of the hill. The hill was quite a long one. Beauty soon got to know the routine and to enjoy it immensely. Immediately she was out of the farm and onto the road, she would gallop up this hill at full speed — churns rattling and me holding the reins — but letting Beauty have her head, because I was enjoying it too.

Beauty loved work, but she was quite difficult to catch. One had to approach her with corn, hoping that she would choose the corn, rather than a continuation of her night's freedom on the fields. As she ate the corn, of course, we would slip a halter over her head. Sometimes she would choose to remain free and gallop away from us, when we were trying to catch her. One day, I drove into Okehampton to buy a galvanised iron cistern. On the way home, whilst still in Okehampton, the trailer went over a bump, the cistern rattled, Beauty took fright and galloped up Okehampton's main street with everybody staring at us. We had a long hill after we left the town and Beauty carried on with her galloping, until she had had enough.

She produced a pretty foal which we sold as soon as it was weaned. We also had another horse named Prince. He was a big, elderly fellow, but very steady and reliable. Beauty, though, often acted on her own initiative. We might be loading something onto the trailer during the afternoon, then turn round and find that the trailer had disappeared. Beauty had decided that it was time for her to go to her stable, for her tea.

One spring evening, Edith and I had a walk to a field where all our sheep were, and we were so gladdened by the sight of the little lambs skipping about and playing together. They would jump up into the air. I took a photo of Edith holding one of the lambs in her arms. Another pleasant evening phenomena, was the singing of the chickens, before they went to sleep. They slept in a rearing house on wheels, which had to be kept shut during the night, because foxes are very partial to a chicken or two. The rearing house would be moved each morning so that the droppings would be falling on fresh grass. Normally, the chickens would be free to roam all day, and they would put themselves to bed. However, if the rearing house had been moved much more than one house length in the morning, then the chickens would be unable to find it, so they would make quite a commotion. I don't know why this happened. It might be that they can't see very well, but they could always see me when I approached them to feed them. No, I think they were very conservative; they knew the exact position of last night's sleeping place and thought that they should be sleeping again in the same spot — not twenty feet further up the field!

Once, when a rearing house caught fire, I gave up all hope of saving it, because it was made of thin wood, and was very dry and was blazing fiercely. At that time, I had a land girl working with me, and she ran to a nearby stream with an empty bucket, which she filled with water, then ran and threw it onto the burning chicken house. The result was that the fire went out immediately and I just stood gaping! That event however, was not on my first farm, but on my second farm, which is the burden of the next chapter.

(Unexpected references to a "lucky fellow" in this chapter are later explained in Part 3, chapter 32.   *A.B.*)

Chapter 28 — MORE TEARS

Having given in my notice to quit my first farm, the time came when I needed to look for a fresh one and one on more productive land. I was now in a position to claim that I was a farmer, and I could demonstrate my capability to any prospective landlord by inviting him to inspect my farm! Farms to let were still scarce, and I was not getting on very well with finding a new farm. One farm that I liked was larger than my present farm, but the owner did not let me have it, due to my existing stock being so much smaller than was needed. Several other farms I saw and visited, I did not like.

However, there was one for sale which was very cheap and on better land. It was a little smaller than mine, being 69 acres. It had much in the way of farm buildings, comparatively. Forestry commission land was adjoining it. Some of the fields were steep and there was no good road into it, only a rough track through the forest. It was very pretty, being in a hollow and having a stream running through it close to the house. If I sold all my stock, I could buy it, but a farm without stock is not much good.

Time was running out! I had put myself in a' jam. There was only one possible way out unless I sold up, and that was to cry to God to get me out of the mess I had put myself into. So, I cried to God: and He heard me! "In my distress I called upon the Lord, and cried unto my God; he heard my voice out of his temple, and my cry came before him, even into his ears". Ps. 18:6. Also, "They cried unto thee, and were delivered: they trusted in thee, and were not confounded". Ps. 22:5. The previous verse says, "Our fathers trusted in thee: they trusted, and thou didst deliver them". There may be hundreds of places in scripture where God intervened to deliver his loved ones; there certainly is a large number. It may be true that many of my readers are likely to need deliverance of one kind or another from all sorts of differing things, serious illness,

77

minor illness, oppression, depression, debt, pride, sin, greed, selfishness, etc., etc. One of the titles given to Jesus is "Deliverer". Rom. 11:26. The most important deliverance is from the penalty and power of sin and this we can all have as soon as we are willing to repent and accept Jesus, our Saviour, into our hearts.

A strange telegram came to my house. It was the first step in God's deliverance of Stanley from his self-made predicament. It said, "Please ring telephone no. ---". I knew nobody with that telephone no. or likely to be associated with that telephone exchange. I did as requested; the voice said, "Are you interested in Farm ---?" I replied, "Yes, I have been trying to buy it". The voice said, "Well, I have bought it". I said, "Thank you for telling me, so that settles that". The reply was, "Come and see me, I don't want to keep the farm". I went to see him, and the position was that he was prepared to sell it to me, for a higher price than what he had paid for it, and he was willing to give me 100% mortgage, enabling me to buy the farm, without using any of my capital. I could therefore move all my stock into this new farm. "Lucky fellow"? No! 'highly blessed', to have a God who is able to deliver me — us! 1 Pet. 5:7 says, "Casting all your care upon Him; for He careth for you". It would seem that there is just no end to the things God has, kept tucked up in His sleeves! Luke 1:37 says, "For with God nothing shall be impossible".

Moving farm stock was great fun, requiring quite a lot of organisation and requiring staff in both places during the process. The two farms were about thirty miles or more apart, but it all went very well.

There was no plumbing whatever on this farm. Water had to be carried up from the nearby stream in milk churns, and the lavatory was a little shed at the bottom of the garden! Cooking was done on an open fire and an oil oven. It was all very primitive, but we managed, and our health was splendid. Much of our washing of hands and faces was done at the stream itself. The stream water was clean, our farm being the first on its route from its source in the forest. The open fire, burning huge logs of wood looked good, but it smoked badly, unless the kitchen door was left open to allow large volumes of cold air to enter the room, so that large volumes of hot air could go up the chimney, taking the smoke with it. Thus, when sitting in front of the open fire, one's front got scorched whilst one's back got frozen.

My main interest at both farms was milk production and rearing cows. I got interested in Jersey cows. I used to think that a cow was a cow, and that they were all much alike as regards behaviour. But I learned that some are much more 'refined' than others and that

Jerseys are very aristocratic, very genteel and sensitive. For a lot of money I was able to buy an elderly Jersey cow and her calf. My first pedigree cow! In the normal way, one cannot allow a calf to be in the shippon where the cows are, as the calf tends to get where it should not be, and the cows tend to object to calves other than their own being near to them. But this Jersey calf would lie quite quietly by itself, and cause no commotion. It would follow us more like a dog than a calf. When I first put the mother in a field, she stood with her nose up in the air for hours and hours before she would eat the grass. I bought a pedigree bull calf, and when he was big enough, I was able to have my first calf, from the old lady. This I had registered, and now I was into breeding pedigree Jerseys, with my own pedigree bull, named "His Royal Highness"!

On the spiritual side, the nearest chapel was some miles away, and quite often I was unable to get to a service, because of the necessary work on the farm, looking after the stock. The parish church was not so far away, and the vicar was a true Bible-believer, but I was not fond of a set repetitive service read from a book! I did actually take the service for the vicar on two occasions: no restrictions whatever were placed on my preaching, but it was essential for me to be dressed up in a surplice! I would have thought, "wear what you like, but preach nothing contrary to scripture"! I really was, through lack of opportunity, of little spiritual value whilst I was farming. But nevertheless I was very happy, the varied life of a farmer out in the open suited me. My conscience did not trouble me, so long as I got to a church whenever I could. I loved my cows immensely.

But, my dear Heavenly Father had other work for me, and he was about to bring my farming career to a close!

Edith had been doing supply teaching, which involved her being away from home and in digs all week. This was to augment our small income. Whilst she enjoyed living on the farm, and taking long walks into the forest with my land girl, nevertheless shopping was difficult, involving a lot of walking and carrying. She never complained, but it seemed only fair to me to say to her, "Edith, whenever you wish me to stop farming just say the word and I will stop". At about this time, one of my best cows who was nearly ready to calf, fell down a steep bank and killed herself. Another, who had calved fairly recently, fell and damaged the nerve in a leg and had to be destroyed. I knew God was showing me something and when I asked Edith if she would like me to give up farming, she said, "Yes". What a wonderful thing it is to have had such an unselfish, loyal wife — Lucky fellow? — no, very highly blessed!

The next step was to sell up. I advertised the farm, and it snowed very hard, a most unusual event in South Devon. However, it was sold, in spite of the snow hiding everything! I had to take my pedigree stock on a long train journey, because there was no market for it locally. Some of the farm implements were sold to the incoming farmer, and I had to lay everything left, out in a field, where an auctioneer could sell it.

It was a painful business, selling up what was giving me such a lot of pleasure and satisfaction. But it was good to experience another side of God's nature. He is to be feared! Psalm 111:10 tells us that 'the fear of the Lord is the beginning of wisdom'. I have said that God has big wide sleeves with all sorts of goodies tucked away in them, but now I must add that He has great big boots!! Adam and Eve must have felt them in action when God pushed them out of the garden of Eden!

Have you, dear reader, been taught to fear God? Do you imagine that it is only the non-christians that need fear God? Acts 5 tells us of a married couple who laid at the apostles' feet part of the price of land they had sold. Surely a commendable action! But, alas, mixed up with the good was the bad; they tried to deceive the apostles over the price, by telling a lie. God's 'boots' came into action and they both lost their lives immediately. In Acts 5:11 we read, "And great fear came upon all the church, and upon as many as heard these things". The next verses tell us of great blessings coming upon the church, great miracles.

Can you imagine what would happen if God were to step into His church today? He would hear someone being called father, who was not Himself; He would see images being worshipped and prayed to. He would find disunity and much ignorance. A vicar of a 'posh' church told me that Jesus is not coming back! But He is coming back, and we should be getting ready to meet Him. Acts 1:11 tells us of the manner of His return.

I was in favour of my going back into industry so as to give Edith some of the comforts of former days. But Edith was in favour of taking on a guest-house. Whilst I knew Edith was very capable domestically, I also noticed that when we had a big number of people for a meal at the farm, it seemed to take a lot out of her.

On the basis upon which we had been running our lives, it certainly was Edith's turn to choose where we lived, and what we did. One thing against my returning to industry was that housing was scarce due to the war. I, personally, was not interested in running a guest-house, but I would help Edith get started, and then I would look for employment as an engineer somewhere nearby. Obviously, at this time I had not fully comprehended my responsibility as a husband.

What is a husband's responsibility? Opinions may differ, but what does the Bible say? This must be important, because the Bible gives us guidance from God on all the main issues of living. It says, "The head of every man is Christ; and the head of the woman is the man; and the head of Christ is God". 1 Cor. 11:3. So there is an ascending order of authority: the woman, the man, Christ, God. Another scripture says, "The husband is the head of the wife, even as Christ is head of the church: and he is the saviour of the body". Eph. 5:23. The next verse says, "Therefore as the church is subject unto Christ, so let the wives be to their own husbands in everything". Eph. 5:24. Another scripture says, "Teach the young women to be sober, to love their husbands, to love their children, to be discreet, chaste, keepers at home, good, obedient to their own husbands, that the word of God be not blasphemed". Titus 2:4, 5. There is here a clear instruction for women to obey their own husbands.

But there is also this, "Likewise, ye husbands, dwell with them according to knowledge, giving honour unto the wife, as unto the weaker vessel, and as being heirs together of the grace of life; that your prayers be not hindered". 1 Pet. 3:7. Note it says, "Giving honour unto the wife, as unto the weaker vessel". The husband is to love his wife, "-- as Christ also loved the church, and gave himself for it". Eph. 5:25. The husbands' love has to be comparable with the love that Christ has for the church! -- which involves, of course, sacrifice!

Too often, it would seem that the wife is the one who either makes the most sacrifices, or alternatively, rules her husband. Both are out of line with the scriptures.

I allowed Edith to take on the responsibility of a guest-house, in full knowledge that it might be a strain on her. Furthermore, we both failed for the second time, in that we did not seek God's mind in this matter.

Chapter 29 — RUNNING A GUEST-HOUSE/HOTEL

We bought 'Endsleigh', a guest-house in Stoke Fleming, on the coast road between Dartmouth and a pretty beach named 'Blackpool Sands'.

We arrived with just one van load of furniture to put into an empty house, with eight bedrooms. The house needed decorating everywhere, both inside and outside, so we had plenty of work on our hands! It was just as well that we were both in good physical condition! We opened it at Easter, when we had our first guests. It was quite a change for us to have electricity, mains water and indoor lavatories!

It was not long before we had knocked down a few dividing walls and replaced the kitchen range with a modern stove, etc., etc. With the money we took from our guests we were able to extend the furnishings so that we could accommodate the steadily increasing number of guests. On one occasion, the furniture for a particular bedroom was a little late in arriving and the guests for that bedroom arrived first! We were taking in this furniture and entertaining the guests in the dining-room all at the same time!

There were plenty of holiday-makers about during our first season, and we did quite well financially, although, of course, our profit had to be sunk into furnishings and equipment, etc. We were so busy that I was needed in the guest-house, so I could not carry out my intention of seeking employment in engineering, at an early date. Indeed, when at last I did seek it, I discovered that there was very little in my line of experience, in that part of England. So I stayed as a guest-house keeper.

One morning when we were fairly full of guests, I set about washing-up the breakfast things, and I was still doing it when the soiled lunch things started to arrive! Edith did the cooking, initially, and that so tied her to the kitchen, that she did not know

Endsleigh Hotel — 1951

who were our guests and who were not. Later we had an elderly lady, whom we called 'Granny', to do the cooking. She was a businesswoman, and was always willing to accept business. One day we did 60 lunches!

'Granny' used to leave things until the last minute, with the result that we would have to rush to avoid being late with meals. So I said to Granny, "When I come in, to help dish up the meals, I want to see you sitting reading the newspaper!" This she did, so that when she heard me coming she would rush for a newspaper and dive into a chair!

Next door to us, and about twenty feet away, was another house. This came on the market. If we were to buy this, we could then join the two houses together with a games' room, and increase the number of our bedrooms from ten to seventeen. The snag was, of course, that it had come on the market rather too soon from our point of view. However, if we did not buy it then, it would be unlikely that we would have another opportunity. We thought that if we were to have another good season then we would be able to finance it, and if the season turned out to be poor, we could sell another house we owned, which was in Liverpool.

We bought this second house, but the next season was poor, so it was necessary to sell the 'back-up' house in Liverpool. Unfortunately, we could not sell it, and once again I found myself in a jam! We had to face the winter with but little money and little income.

Some christian friends said to me, "You should cast your burdens on the Lord". (1 Pet. 5:7.) Well, how does one do that? I didn't know. Next, Edith became ill; her stomach became swollen and it looked as though it would be serious. Now, I had both the financial worry and the illness. I said to the Lord, "I can't take this, it is too much for me". That was what the Lord was waiting for me to say! I found myself sliding out, as it were, from beneath the burden.

Edith recovered from her swollen stomach, but before long she had to spend long periods resting quietly in a nearby chalet. It soon became apparent that Edith could no longer take her place in the hotel, due to failing health, and that I had to decide whether to run it without her or sell up, and go back into industry, which I had left nearly twelve years previously. You may recollect that we had embarked on the hotel business without first seeking God's will. Also, that I had failed as a husband, in not taking my proper place of responsibility for my dear wife, as her head. Now, of course, I was faced with the consequences of those two errors.

I could, of course, run the hotel without her help, but it did not seem right, because the hours were very long and she would see me very little. No! it seemed right for me to retrace my steps and go back into industry.

Chapter 30 — SPIRITUAL BLESSINGS

During our early days in Endsleigh we heard some lively chorus singing coming from somewhere in the village. It drew us like a magnet, and we found it was coming from an upper room called Sander's Meeting Room. It was being used by the section of the church known as the 'Brethren'. We joined them, and received much help due to their great respect for the Bible.

Two christian lads were baptised in the sea; it drew quite a crowd of spectators, who remained whilst one of the lads followed his baptism by giving a gospel address. My own father, who was not a regular church or chapelgoer, remained throughout the witness.

At a time when it seemed, for various reasons, impossible for me to leave Endsleigh, I received an invitation to a conference on Revival. My wife was in bed ill, and I had not the needed money. God performed miracles and I went, full of gratitude to God for enabling me to go to this conference, which was in Weston-super-Mare.

The first session opened with an announcement that, "There will now be an opportunity for testimony, by those who have been able to get here only through miracles". I thought, 'fine', I would be able to tell the folks how money, owing to me for nearly thirty years and given up as lost, was returned just in time for this conference, without me asking for it. However, there were so many other testimonies of miraculous help, that I did not have the chance to give mine!

Before hearing of the conference, I had already taken to heart the scripture which says, "confess your faults, one to another". It was quite painful having to confess to the church that I was guilty of doing something which I hated, known as 'exclusivism', which means shutting out — cold-shouldering — christians having beliefs a little different from our own beliefs. At the conference we were encouraged to confess our faults. Many did so. I got up and said, "I am in a worse state than any of you, I don't know of any unconfessed fault, yet I believe I still have them". I sat down and it seemed to me as though God whispered to me, 'Pride'. I silently confessed pride to God with repentance. Next we all sang a hymn and, as I had not been able to sing in tune, nor to appreciate music, nor to appreciate poetry, hymn singing had given me no pleasure. But now, God worked another miracle. I enjoyed singing that hymn so much that tears ran down my face and I knew that there was nothing in this life that could give one more pleasure than praising God, when the spirit is 'fired' by God. The pleasure had nothing to do with my musical ability, which was almost nil, and nothing to do with poetry. I was not familiar with the words we sang and I did not remember any of them! No, it must have been God's spirit — the Holy Ghost — singing through my spirit.

After I returned home I found that I had more power, more confidence; bringing to mind that the early disciples had given to them the promise of power, in Acts 1:8. They were told to tarry in the city of Jerusalem until they were endued with power from on high, as recorded in Luke 24:49. They had been taught by Jesus; they had the necessary head knowledge for service, and they had the needed authority given to them, John 20:21; in addition they had the Holy Ghost, John 20:22. But still they were not ready for service, they needed something more; they needed to tarry until they were baptised with the Holy Ghost. Which, of course, happened at the feast of Pentecost, as described in Acts 2.

I personally, received the Holy Ghost when I was converted, but now, some fifteen years later, I became conscious of power for the first time. Lots of power? No! Just a little power! We needed a piano in Endsleigh because we had a gospel effort, with a visiting evangelist. There were no piano shops in the village of Stoke Fleming, but as we, the leader and I, walked up the hill together towards the church, I just felt that we would obtain a piano, and I'd have been surprised if God did not supply one. The first man I spoke to, telling him of our need, sold us a piano! Praise the Lord! Some christians believe, nowadays, that the Baptism of the Spirit takes place at conversion, and they also believe that the gifts of the Spirit ceased with the first century. I suppose that one of the biggest causes of division in the church, lies here. It would seem that satan must be involved in this, because otherwise we would be seeking the truth and would be paying but little attention to denominational tradition. We would also be able to recognise prejudice for what it is.

Shock No.13: is God giving to a man with almost NO musical ability, so much joy in singing a hymn that tears run down his face, and he becomes aware that there cannot be a greater joy in this life, than that which he was then experiencing. Clearly a miracle! Psalm 16:11 tells us that in the presence of God is fulness of joy!

At the same conference at which I had received this blessing, there were other testimonies of note. One of the two organisers of the conference was an Anglican vicar; a very gifted man, well educated, eloquent and musical. He told us that one day he stood in front of his congregation and he thought to himself, 'I have a lot of cabbages in front of me, there is little life in them and they are a pretty incapable bunch. I know what I will do; I will get a revivalist to come and wake them up'. This he did, but as the revivalist ministered the word of God, he himself became convicted of sin, and he confessed to his church that he was hard and unloving, proud, etc. Actually he was those things no longer! Confession had changed him into a loving, humble vicar.

Another testimony was given by an Irish lady, in her thirties I would think. She had read a book on revival, which she thought was good, so she lent it to her friends, who acted on its teaching and became revived, but she, the owner of the book, had not become revived. So she reread the book, acted on its teaching and became revived. She said the experience she had was like being converted all over again, and she became full of joy, so much so that she had to leave her desk, and fellow typists, and hide where she could have a good sing to God. Note that she was not a teenager, but a mature woman!

The Bible tells us that Jesus came "that they might have life, and that they might have it more abundantly". (John 10:10). Also that 'joy' is one of the nine fruits of the Holy Ghost. Gal. 5:22.

I have come across people who deny that there is a second blessing.

May these testimonies reach some such; and may they become willing to accept this evidence! The disciples were not willing to believe the reports that Jesus had risen from the tomb. We read, "He appeared unto the eleven as they sat at meat, and upbraided them with their unbelief and hardness of heart, because they believed not them which had seen Him after he was risen". Mk. 16:14. There are those who don't believe lots of things that are written in the Bible; Jesus said to Thomas, "and be not faithless, but believing" John 20:27b. "Take heed, brethren, lest there be in any of you an evil heart of unbelief, in departing from the living God". Heb. 3:12.

Chapter 31 — CONCLUSION TO PART 2

There is much more to be written, covering the period from 1953, when we left Endsleigh, up to the time when this was written. But there is so much, that perhaps it would be better to continue the account in a third part of the book. (In which, as is mentioned in chapter 27, we learn more about this enigmatic 'Lucky Fellow'.)

Part 3

FROM 1953 ONWARDS

Chapter 32 — THE RETURN TO INDUSTRY

I secured an interview for a job near London. I did not get that job but the firm paid my fare, anyway. Whilst I was in the London area, I called upon the Plessey Co., in Ilford, and I was taken on as a Design Engineer in their Aircraft Electrical Division. They needed an engineer to design aircraft relays, as it happened, and this was right up my own street, for I had spent many years on relays whilst in Liverpool.

Selling the hotel was not easy. We had to sell the second house separately, and leave someone to run the first house, until such time as it was sold. I believe it was God who guided me to an employer needing an engineer knowledgeable on relays.

Whilst we were running the hotel I had bought a large car for taking guests for trips out to Dartmoor. It was a seven-seater landaulette(!) with a glass partition between the driver and his passengers. We took this to our new home near London. There was, as yet, no garage and the car used to stand on a concrete base, which in due course would be part of the garage. The engine was not running very well, and the fault was distortion of the cylinder head. I just did not want to pay the cost of having the cylinder head reground, and so I bought some files, then set about filing the head flat. It might have seemed a bit ambitious, but it was successful and now the engine would run smoothly, at remarkably low speeds.

The ratchet on the handbrake was faulty, so it became customary, on stopping the engine, to leave the car in bottom gear. For some reason, now obscure, the self-starter was also out of action, and it was necessary to use the starting handle, which was always left in position as part of the car.

One morning, shortly after I had rejuvenated the engine, I gave the starting handle just one pull up. The engine started beautifully and, as the car was still in gear, it came towards me. Backing off the concrete onto the garden, I fell down with the car still coming towards me. It was apparent that one of its front wheels was going over me, so I got ready to take its not-inconsiderable weight.

After running over me, it encountered a small apple tree, which, of course, brought it to a halt. I found I could not rise because of the front axle, which had pushed my knee into the soft earth, and thus was holding it in the ground. It was not hurting, it was merely trapping it in the soft soil.

My daughter, Dawn, saw what had happened, and she called out to her mother, "Daddy is under the car". Edith thought, 'Daddy is often under the car', and she took no notice. A neighbour on one side learnt what had happened and, although he was weak on his legs he ran down his own garden to get a jack, so that he could lift the car. The neighbour on the other side came down with a flask of brandy, but her hands were so shaky, that it was really she who needed the brandy, because as far as I knew, I was not hurt; and I was not frightened — I was far too busy endeavouring to take the weight to be frightened.

The jack proved useless, because, instead of the car rising, the jack sank into the soft soil. So it was decided to get the aid of the fire service who would have a big jack. Presently the fire bells were ringing and firemen were coming into the house, saying, "Where's the fire?"

They had a big jack, and very soon my leg was free of pressure from the axle. I got up thinking I was uninjured, but I could feel a little hurting in my chest. An ambulance had arrived, so I went to the hospital for X-rays. No bones were broken, so I was allowed to go home provided I stayed in bed for a few days. A friend who attended the same church as me was, I think, the first to say to me, "Lucky fellow!", although others did later say the same thing. The accident happened on Tuesday morning, Jan. 12th, 1954, and I started to write this account two days later. The Bible says, "Are not two sparrows sold for a farthing? and one of them shall not fall to the ground without your Father". Matt. 10:29. Another scripture says, "He careth for you". 1 Pet. 5:7. The context of the first scripture is teaching given to Jesus' twelve disciples. He was not talking to the world at large, nor was He addressing the religious people, the Pharisees. The second scripture lies in the context of God's people and, similarly, it is not necessarily applicable to those who are not His.

We make a mistake when we fail to recognise the conditions associated with the very many promises in the Bible. I used to think that God would answer all prayers, and I would be puzzled when I did not seem to have an answer to my prayers. Then I had no knowledge of the conditions to be fulfilled before prayer is answered. The condition which is most important is that we need to be 'born again'. Another is that we must be free from unconfessed sin, and yet another is that our prayers must be in line with His will.

I had a little sister aged about ten, of whom I was very fond and I always imagined that we would one day live together. She was physically weak and had meningitis, so I prayed hard that she would live, but she died. I was not then a christian in the sense of being born-again, and I had no light on God's will in the matter. I suppose I would be about fifteen or sixteen at the time. Prayer is a wonderful privilege, but we do need to know all the conditions that have to be fulfilled.

We joined a free evangelical church with a gifted pastor. His gift was particularly in evangelism; one could take an unsaved friend to that church and be fairly certain that the way of salvation would be faithfully proclaimed. The church grew rapidly in numbers and it soon became necessary to put seats in the aisles. Conversions and baptisms of believers were common occurrences. The pastor did all the preaching, also he took the midweek Bible study, which was very well attended. But one day he was taken ill suddenly, and was unable to come to the Bible study. The secretary announced to the assembled company — "We won't be able to have our Bible study this evening, because the pastor is unable to attend". It seemed to me rather sad if, after years of listening to sermons and doing Bible study, we were still so dependent on one man.

The Bible says, "Jesus Christ — hath made us kings and priests unto God". Revn. 1:5, 6. The context is John's salutation to the seven churches, and not to the pastors of the churches — if any! Peter, on writing to — 'the strangers scattered throughout Pontus, Galatia, etc.' says, "Ye — are built up a spiritual house, an holy priesthood --". 1 Pet. 2:5. Hence the assembled company that evening was, according to scripture, a company of kings and priests and part of an holy priesthood.

The convention, or tradition, evidently rendered the priests rather ineffective in ministering to one another. Note how contrary this was to my experience in the little city mission when various ones ministered on the evils of smoking! (see chapter 26). We need to check our organisation, to see if we have limited the Holy Spirit in His use of various people in diverse places.

My job in industry was going on alright, despite a twelve-year gap. When I had a difficult design to do, I would pray to God, and it would work out alright. God is a wonderful engineer! My hours seemed very easy in comparison with the hotel. I had every evening free and all day Saturday and Sunday. This proved very valuable for christian work, and I seemed to be able to do so much more christian work now, than I was able to do in the hotel, all due to this greatly increased free time. I lived close enough to the factory to be able to get home at my lunch-time, but quite often I chose to have my lunch in my place of work, so that I could talk to my colleagues about spiritual things.

Billy Graham came to Harringay, the year after I moved and I became one of his 'counsellors'. During the training lessons for this we were encouraged to learn scriptures off by heart. In fact, we were not allowed to counsel before we had learnt four specific scriptures. Since I had a bad memory, I was rather slow in memorising scripture, but I came to find it a very valuable thing to do.

There were also some training classes for those willing to take on more than counselling by looking after the new converts, for a period. These classes were very well attended, and I found them most useful, in fact very beneficial, as you will see in the next chapter.

The Factory Fellowship with "Lucky Fellow!" *chariot — 1954*

Chapter 33 — THE FACTORY FELLOWSHIP

These 'Follow Up' classes were so popular that they had to be duplicated. They were run by Lorne Sanny, the man in charge of the counsellors' training classes. Amongst the things he told us was that a hen does not have more chicks than she can look after. Implying that we should not have more new christians, under our wings, than we can look after. I came to the understanding that looking after christians, is really 'pastoring' — although that name wasn't used in the classes.

Since I thought the teaching received to be so good, I told myself that I had better put it into practice. So, one day, I went to one of my colleagues in the office saying something like, "Are you interested in spiritual things, because if you are, I would like to have a chat with you? We can go out into the country in my car". He was quite willing, and I had prepared myself with the scriptures necessary for leading him to Jesus. The preliminary, as we had been taught, was to probe in order to find out where the 'candidate' stood. This I did, and lo and behold! I found that he was already a christian, and had been such for about a year. This rather took the wind out of my sails. Still I said, "Well, as far as I can see, you need now to be baptised, but don't take it from me. I will lend you my concordance, and you can look up your own scriptures on baptism, and then it won't be me who is telling you what to do". It took him only a few days to come to the conclusion that he should be baptised, but it was about three weeks before he became willing to be baptised. In the meantime, of course, he was fighting with himself against taking this step of obedience. He was baptised in the Free Evangelical Church to which I belonged.

There was a Methodist young man in the office who was keen on evangelism. We met very soon after my arrival, and we formed the habit of meeting together at lunch-time. In fact, without any planning, we were a christian fellowship of two christians! I suppose the newly-baptised young man would make a third. I can't remember exactly the order of things, but before long, our fellowship grew in numbers. We would take people to evangelistic meetings, get them saved, and look after them. We appointed a 'pastor' to each new christian, who would have a word or two with his charge each day. The 'pastor' would usually be rather inexperienced, but he could always go to more experienced 'pastors' when he wished, for advice.

Once a week we had a meeting at lunch-time and we arranged that each person in the fellowship, in turn, was responsible for the meeting. He or she could run it as they wished, and if they did not want to run it they could appoint somebody else, willing to take their place. Our numbers had grown to about ten, and it was very remarkable that there was never an occasion, when a person fought shy of taking the meeting. They may have been converted only a few weeks, but nevertheless they'd be willing to do their bit. I remember that on one occasion it became the turn for a Salvation Army lass to lead us. She brought along her own church handbook on doctrine and told us that baptism and communion were not required. We all said that the book was wrong, and that the Bible does require baptism and communion. She seemed very surprised. I invited her to my house where we talked about baptism. At the end of the eveining she said to me, "I don't agree with you". But it was only a few days later that she told me that I was quite right! But it took a long time before she was willing to be baptised. However, she was baptised in the local swimming-baths!

In the main factory about three or four miles away, they had a weekly prayer meeting in a nearby hall. We used to attend this initially, when we were very few in numbers and had not yet started our own weekly meetings. One day, one young man prayed that we might not be a hindrance to one another. I thought that was a bit weak, so I prayed that we might be a help to one another, and proceeded to read scriptures on baptism. The leader told me that it was very wrong of me to have mentioned baptism, because there would be some there that did not believe in baptism.

I thought the leader must be one such, and I arranged to go to his house; my object being to minister to him on baptism. I went, and much to my surprise, he had been baptised as a believer. What had happened was that he had changed his denomination, and he was following his new denomination, rather than the scripture. In consequence of this experience, I decided that our little fellowship would be run differently. It would not confine its activity to prayer only, and everybody would be quite free to say what they believed, and we would have a time for discussion. The little salvationist, for she was very small in stature, took no offence at the rest of us disagreeing with what she told us. She was just surprised, and ultimately she received the benefit. It is worth recording that on no occasion did anybody take offence when someone or other disagreed with them. There was no need for us to be afraid of one another and we were not.

Once we had a catholic to address us. He spoke on meditation, advocating it, praising it. We said to him afterwards that meditation could only be of value if we were meditating on helpful things. He spoke as though meditation was always helpful. There are I think, non-christian religions where folks are encouraged to make their minds blank in meditation. I would think this would give satan an opportunity to pop into the mind what ought not to be there. Surely one could, and should not, meditate on robbing a bank! I felt the meeting was well worthwhile, because it provided the corrective influence that was needed.

A few years ago I was at an interdenominational renewal meeting. It was time for a catholic mass. The presiding bishop was almost in tears because he could not allow his protestant brothers and sisters to take the elements. I longed to say, "Why not?" but I was feeling the absurdity of the situation too much to trust myself to speak! If only we all would try to follow the scriptures, instead of a man, I expect our denominational barriers would soon melt away. Some of us, I expect, do not really want to know the truth, we are happy with our 'own' denomination and we don't want to change. Are we *that* silly that we don't know the difference between the taste of wine and the taste of blood? Or are we so silly as to believe that when Jesus took bread and said, "This is my body", that he meant it literally? Dear reader, may I encourage you to be very loving, but very bold, when you meet error.

The man I spoke to about baptism was named Fred King. Shortly afterward two people were converted, a man named Leonard, and I have forgotten the name of the woman, (it was Gwen). I said to Fred, "Go and talk to Leonard about baptism". I thought it would be good to start Fred off on 'pastoring'. Fred did this, and found that Leonard was quite willing to be baptised, but he wanted to have a word with his vicar first.

I saw a danger in this, so I went to Leonard saying, "You must first make yourself thoroughly familiar with all the scriptures on baptism, before you see your vicar". This Leonard did, and when his vicar tried to persuade him against being baptised, Leonard stood firm and the man could do nothing with him. In the end, the vicar admitted that his own children had not been christened!

G

The lady secretary of the section in which I was employed was a very worldly-looking woman with lots of make-up and nail varnish, and was a heavy smoker. When I talked to her about Jesus, she said, "There is no hope for me". I said, "Why not?" and she replied that she was too bad. I told her that nobody was so bad, but what Jesus could save them, and that the scripture said, "Though your sins be as scarlet, they shall be as white as snow". Isa. 1:18. I encouraged her to go to Wembley Stadium to hear Billy Graham preach, and I encouraged her to respond to his message by going out to the front when he invited folks so to do.

She went, and took her dear old mother with her; and they both responded to the message. This was on a Thursady and the next day she told me what they had done. I arranged for her and her mother to be at the church I attended, on the next Sunday. After the service I took them down to the front of the church to show them where they would be baptised on the following Sunday. The pastor, seeing what was happening, came up saying, "We shall be having some baptisms next week, perhaps you would like to see them". I butted in with, "Oh no, they are going to be baptised next Sunday, not merely watch a baptism". And they were both of them baptised.

Spiritual growth under the ministry of 'daily meals' was so rapid that this lady was able to bring her husband to the Lord, after only a few weeks. They have both been much used by God in soul winning, and the husband became the minister of baptist churches — one quite a big church. Leonard also made good spiritual progress. He wanted to become a missionary and he left the firm to go to a Bible college. The young woman, whose name I have forgotten (q.v.), joined a good evangelical church in which she got baptised. We thought that, since she had joined a 'good' church, she would not need the daily ministration that we were giving to the others. But after a few months we noticed that this young woman had not grown as fast as did the others. Hence, we changed our policy and decided that in future we would look after every new christian, no matter how good we might judge their church to be.

During the 'follow up' training classes we were taught to give frequent 'meals'! A new-born physical baby would not thrive on one large meal given once a week. The baby needs frequent meals of easily digestible food. There are other similarities between the physical and the spiritual; a physical baby needs warmth and personal attention.

It needs washing. It needs correction and it also needs exercise. I suppose this need for spiritual exercise is rarely appreciated. We too often expect people to grow spiritually without it.

It seemed that in our 'Factory Fellowship' people grew in six months about as much as they would in a 'good' church in six years. The reason would seem to be the opportunity for exercise as well as the daily ministry. Most of us had joined 'good' churches, but nevertheless we all agreed after a while, that our worship in our factory meetings was deeper and better than what it was in our 'good' churches.

Dawn   Gillian

''The Lucky Fellow's'' very loving daughters,
Dawn and Gillian (ch. 43)

Chapter 34 — WHY ALL THIS BAPTISM?

Concerning baptism, I had encouraged two men to search the scriptures on this subject, but I had never done that myself! So, I got down to the job with my concordance; and it seemed that from then onwards God frequently used me to minister on that subject.

Prevailing customs vary; many churches baptise babies, as well as adults. Others will only baptise adults. Yet others will only baptise those who have been 'born-again', 'converted'. There is also a tendency to leave it for the 'born-again' one to discover for himself that he ought to be baptised. The baptism of babies is a very common practice; many believe that the baby becomes 'saved' thereby. If the baby should be physically weak, some will hasten the baptism in case the baby were to die unbaptised.

My wife, who was not converted at the time, wanted to have our first baby, Jillian, baptised. So I asked my vicar to give to me the scripture for the baptism of babies. He referred me to the Philippian jailer of Acts 16:33, saying that all that were in the house were baptised, and that there must have been babies in the house. I thought about this and I had to admit that only a minority of houses had babies in them. The majority did not. It seemed incredible that a doctrine could be build on such a weak assumption. Later, I noticed that in the next verse, 34, it say that all his house believed in God. A baby could not believe in God, so there is an indication that there was *not* a baby in his house. I have read other works on the subject, but there was always made an assumption, which I was not prepared to confuse with the plain statements of scripture. There are no plain statements of scripture which authorise the baptism of babies, nor indeed of adults unless they have become believers. Peter, at the end of his first sermon, says, ''Repent, and be baptised every one of you in the name of Jesus Christ for the remission of sins, and ye shall receive the gift of

100

the Holy Ghost". Acts 2:38. Salvation, in the scripture, is not based on any religious ceremony, but on heart belief. (John 3:16). The Ethiopian eunuch said to Philip, "See, here is water; what doth hinder me to be baptised?" And Philip said, "If thou believest with all thine heart, thou mayest". Acts 8:36, 37. In some modern versions v.37 is omitted, why? Jesus commanded his disciples to teach all nations, baptising them. Matt. 28:19.

There are records in scripture of many baptisms, they always follow belief. For example, when Peter preached to Cornelius, and his kinsmen and friends, he said, "Whosoever believeth in him shall receive remission of sins". Acts 10:43. The account goes on to say that the Holy Ghost fell on all them that heard the word, and that they spake with tongues. Then in the last verse of the chapter, he, Peter, commanded them to be baptised. Acts 10:48. Note please that Peter *commanded* them to be baptised, he did not leave it for them to discover that they ought to be baptised. He did not leave it for them to reach a measure of maturity first. No, in scripture, baptism follows belief immediately. When Saul was converted, he was three days without sight as he went on his way to Damascus, where he was to receive ministry from Ananias and to have his sight restored to him. Acts 9:9—12. When he arrived, Ananias healed his sight and said, "And now why tarriest thou? arise, and be baptised, and wash away thy sins, calling on the name of the Lord". Acts 22:16. Note the words, "why tarriest thou?" He had only been converted three days, but evidently his baptism was a bit late!

There are, of course, some strange ideas about the significance of baptism. Many think of it as an initiation ceremony into a denomination and sometimes when people change their denomination, they are required to be baptised a second time. The scripture says, "Know ye not, that as many of us as were baptised into Jesus Christ were baptised into his death?". Rom. 6:3. We should be baptised into Jesus Christ, and not into any denomination; and the significance is, in symbolic form, entering into the death of Christ and into the resurrection of Christ. The words of scripture are, "Therefore we are buried with him by baptism into death: that like as Christ was raised up from the dead by the glory of the Father, even so we also should walk in newness of life". Rom. 6:4. So, I repeat, baptism represents burial with Christ and resurrection with Christ. It is a ceremony of burial and resurrection in symbolic form.

Only a true believer can wish to be buried with Christ, and certainly only a true believer can be 'raised up from the dead ---- (to) walk in newness of life'.

Many think that the symbolism does not need a lot of water.

That the sprinkling of a little water is sufficient, but remember the words of scripture were 'buried with' (Christ). John the Baptist was, "baptising in Aenon near to Salim, because there was much water there". John 3:23.

When the Ethiopian eunuch was baptised we read, "and they went down both into the water, both Philip and the eunuch; --- And when they were come up out of the water, ---". Acts 8:38, 39. They went 'down into' and they came 'up out of'.

In my experience, when candidates 'go down into', and 'come up out of', there is often a very strong atmosphere created; and sometimes the candidate will say, 'I wish I could be baptised all over again!' I remember that when a young man was baptised in the sea at Blackpool Sands in Devon, the crowd on the beach were much affected and stayed on while this same lad preached to them after he was dressed. There was quite a write-up about it in the local newspaper, and I think it used the words 'visibly moved', to describe the effect on the crowd. A few years ago, a blind minister wanted to be baptised, and met with great difficulty. Some would baptise him, so long as he would change his denomination, which he was unwilling to do. He was a congregationalist and he did not wish to sever his connection with that body — who had paid for his training. Eventually, he was baptised in the local swimming-baths.

Going back to my daughter Jillian, I decided I could allow her to be 'christened' in the parish church, but that I would demonstrate my disagreement by being outside, rather than inside during the ceremony. As I was holding all sorts of offices in that church, I expected there to be quite a rumpus, for I was rebelling against one of its foundational ceremonies. Much to my surprise, nobody said a word about my absence from the christening!

May one be baptised for a second time when the first baptism was not correct? We have the case in scripture where certain disciples had not received the Holy Ghost. Acts 19:2. Paul said to them, "Unto what then were ye baptised? And they said, Unto John's baptism. Then said Paul, John verily baptised with the baptism of repentance, saying unto the people, that they should believe on him which should come after him, that is, on Christ Jesus. When they heard this, they were baptised in the name of the Lord Jesus". Acts 19:3, 4, 5. Their initial baptism had been incorrect, since the name of Jesus Christ was omitted. But surely, any baptism of unbelievers would be equally incorrect, because they are not 'dying with Christ', nor being 'resurrected with Christ'. Nothing is happening to them, the symbolism of burial is quite meaningless. Furthermore, sprinkling with a little water could hardly represent burial, even if the candidate was a believer.

After her conversion, Edith herself was baptised in 'much water', together with most of the congregation in the little mission near Liverpool.

Some people try to avoid mentioning baptism because of the differences in belief. Since the scripture would have us all saying the same things, and being of one mind (1 Cor. 1:10), it follows that we need to study and talk about baptism. Whilst I have been used to bring many to baptism, there is just one man whom I never did succeed in persuading to be baptised. I believe he knew that he should be baptised, but was unwilling to face the frowns that would come from his denomination. I offered to go through the scriptures with him, but he would not let me do so. This man lost out as regards respect from the other members of the factory fellowship; all of whom had been baptised in 'much water'.

What is the right time to mention baptism? It is at the same time as preaching on the way of salvation. Peter said, "Repent, and be baptised", Acts 2:38. I found that when I did this, then folks would come up to me after they got converted saying, "I suppose I ought to be baptised", and all I needed to say was, "Yes". There was no struggling and delaying as so often occurs when baptism crops up months or even years after their conversion.

Life becomes so much easier when we stick closely to scripture! and get away from the fear of man. "The fear of man bringeth a snare: but whoso putteth his trust in the Lord shall be safe". Prov. 29:25.

Chapter 35 — A HOUSE SUNDAY SCHOOL

Our house was about a mile or more from the Free Evangelical Church and in between was a main road, not safely crossable by small children. So that children living near us could not safely go to the Evangelical church for Sunday school. Also, there was no other church with a Sunday school near to us.

It was apparent that we should have a Sunday school in our house, as an auxiliary to the Sunday school in the Free Evangelical Church. The superintendent was a very humble man whom I admire so very much that I would like to place his name on record; it was Fred Lutkins.

He came to our immediate housing area to recruit children for the Sunday school which was to be in our house. The response was so great, that he had to stop after he had been in just two short roads! We then bought some small folding chairs for the little ones, and we kept them stacked under the stairs when not in use. A lady used to come each week to play the piano for us. The children were of various ages — I suppose about 4—12. The older ones used to look after the younger ones, taking off their coats and putting them on the stairs, and later helping them to dress before going home.

We would all be in the back room for singing etc., and then we would divide up into two groups, with the older ones in the front room. There was something very lovely about that Sunday school! The parents were very appreciative, and even some, who were not religious, were willing to have the school in their own house when we were away on holiday. The superintendent left us quite free to run it just as we wished, and when there were special events on at the Evangelical church, such as Sunday school anniversary, we could join with them or not as we pleased. It was most usual for us to join them, loading our big car with, I suppose, two loads of children. One of the older boys was named Stanley! I wonder if what I am now writing will ever get into his hands?

Chapter 36 — "ENLARGE THE PLACE OF THY TENT"

After a few years, we needed to move house because Edith's aunt was no longer fit to live alone. She could look after herself, but she had need to live close to a relative, and Edith was her only relative. Our present house was quite small.

Edith saw an advert for a house, which had been divided into two flats and which was situated a few miles away in Ilford, the very town in which we had both been brought up. The price was low and we thought that this house must consequently be in the less desirable part of the town. However, we discovered that it was in a good part of the town close to Cranbrook Park, and close to where we both had lived before we were married.

We expected it to be in a bad state of repair, since the price was low. But to our amazement, it had been repainted outside, redecorated right through inside, and fitted with new tiled fireplaces. During the war the council had taken it over, and had now had to put it into good order before releasing it for sale.

It was ideal for us! Another remarkable thing was, that it had not been advertised in Ilford — where it was situated — but in Romford, the area in which we were at present living. In Ilford there was a lady who was looking for a house just like that, and she was puzzled as to why we had found it and not her. "But my God shall supply all your need . ." Philippians 4:19.

Lucky Fellow! Yes, once more I had come face to face with a loving God. But God has promised to bless us, just as he blessed Abraham, if we will be obedient. The scripture that I have in mind is, "And if ye be Christ's, then are ye Abraham's seed, and heirs according to the promise". Gal. 3:29. That means that we inherit from Abraham the blessings God promised to Abraham's seed (descendants). I have not many spiritual children, but I do have a large number of spiritual grandchildren.

Before Billy Graham came to London in 1954, I used to attend mid-week meetings in a methodist church close to my home. I was invited to speak at one of these meetings, and I chose as the title of my address: "The Scriptures of Truth", because I thought there was a need to teach that the Bible is true, to that congregation. Their minister was present; he was an elderly and rather loveable man, and he told me after the meeting that he was not surprised I had spoken on that subject! We talked about kings, and I mentioned how wrong it was of the children of Israel to set up a king. It was then that he said to me, "I envy you your faith". I felt so sorry for him, partly because faith is so important in his occupation, and partly because he was so much older than I was.

The words, "Scriptures of truth" were not spoken originally by man, but by an angel. Dan. 10:21. The Bible warns us against those things that would destroy our faith. "Beware lest any man spoil you through philosophy and vain deceit, after the tradition of men, after the rudiments of the world, and not after Christ". Col. 2:8. Also — "O Timothy, keep that which is committed to thy trust, avoiding profane and vain babblings, and oppositions of science falsely so called". 1 Tim. 6:20.

Note that it says, "oppositions of science falsely so called". There is no opposition from true science. Those that imagine there is are not scientific. I once read a book which sets out to destroy the Bible by reasoning, and I found that the reasoning employed was faulty, and that conclusions were being arrived at that were illogical. For example, if two accounts differ, it does not necessarily follow that there is any error; they can both be right whilst being different because they each mention different aspects or different details.

I remember Billy Graham saying once, that when he came to believe the Bible he found he had more power in his ministry. I think he said that he had to unlearn some of the things he had learned during his theological training!

Chapter 37 — HOLIDAYS IN EUROPE

It was my friend Derwent Sharpe who first took us on a holiday into Europe. We went to Switzerland, spending a week in Wilderswil, near to Interlaken, and a week in Altdorf, about fifty miles further east. We travelled in Derwent's car, a 1600cc Hillman Minx, flying from Southend to Calais. The cost of flying the one-ton car, needing staff to load it, was far less than the cost of the quarter-ton of passengers who had loaded themselves!

We decided to spend the Sunday resting after the long motor journey. We were sitting in the hotel garden, when I jumped over a narrow flowerbed to land on the path the other side. The path had small loose stones and as I landed, I sprained my ankle! That rather curtailed my walking, but it by no means ruined the holiday. There was always so much to see that was grand in the way of scenery; and whilst the other members of the party went exploring, I could read a book which I found very interesting, the life of Spurgeon. We found the mountain scenery to be very grand, very much grander than in Britain, and well worth the extra distance of travel. I formed the impression that the staff operating the mountain railway were rather proud of their jobs.

At Altdorf, I came to the same conclusion after watching a team who were emptying dustbins! In the hotel, there was a young girl — perhaps 11 or 12 years of age — dusting the sides of the stairs. She also gave me the impression that she was enjoying the job. Manual work can be a great source of enjoyment and satisfaction. I think that in Great Britain there is sometimes an overemphasis on mental accomplishments.

--------------- Jesus, of course, was a carpenter! ----------------

On the second Sunday we drove down to the waters' edge of Lake Lucerne and there had our little worship service. My friend Derwent was a choir master and organist and so was able to help us

— me — keep in tune. But isn't it grand to have praise to God bubbling up from inside us? The psalmist says, "Make a joyful noise unto God". Ps. 66:1, Ps. 81:1, Ps. 95:2, Ps. 98:4 and Ps. 100:1. We don't need to be very musical to make a joyful noise. What would it be like in church, if we all took to heart those scriptures . . . and arrived with all sorts of things with which to make a noise; trumpets, drums, whistles, etc.!

Another year, we had a similar holiday in the Dolomites of northern Italy. We found the roads there to be remarkably free from traffic although it was the holiday season. I remember once, as we approached the town of Cortina at evening time, I stood in the middle of the road and made a cine-film of the mountains and the clouds, all of which were of a pink hue, touched by the setting sun. I was not standing in the way of the traffic, because there was no traffic!

Yet another holiday was at Lake Garda. I was very impressed by the quality of the roads in difficult places. On the west side of Garda the mountainside comes down to the lake very steeply, and the road is in a tunnel running parallel to the lakeside, with window openings every 30 or 50 yards to provide light and ventilation. At one place the road is on a shelf built out from the mountain. I was surprised at the amount of enterprise that must have been involved. We had rented a flat in a block of about eight flats, with its own private swimming-pool. It was here that I saw my first praying mantis and my first scorpion.

We visited Venice where I had a swim in water I expected to be warm at the Lido, but it wasn't. On the way home from Gardone we spent two nights amongst the high mountains in a place, which I think was called Meiringen. We visited the Susten Pass, and we discovered that we were being deceived about distances and the size of the mountains. They were much bigger than they looked. We also visited the Rhone Glacier. It was warmer inside the glacier, where there was a tunnel cut into the ice, than it was outside; the reason being that outside there was a strong, cold wind blowing. We had three drivers on this holiday, and we used a bigger car, a Humber Super-Snipe. Also we flew to Ostend rather than to Calais, because we found that the roads going east through Belgium were better than those through the North of France.

Another holiday was spent in a Swiss chalet, 2,000ft above sea-level in a hamlet near to Villars, about twelve miles from Montreux. We went in June, and at that time of year there could have been snow at 2,000ft, but we had lovely sunshine, I think all of the time. We were surprised to find that crocuses were all over some of the higher ground, and that the grass did not come until the crocuses were dying down. Wild flowers generally, in Switzerland, are much more abundant than in Great Britain. A hay field, close to the chalet, had no grass; it was nothing but wild flowers. I remember a churchyard in which there was no grass, but lots and lots of small begonias.

We often spent one night in a little German town named Emmendingen, on the road between Strasbourg and Freiburg. There are large-sized vessels of flowers beside the roadside, good fountains, and they manage to illuminate the roadway at night without there being any glare from the lights. I know of no other place where the lights are so hidden. We ought to send our streetlighting engineers there to see how it's done! Being both an engineer and a motorist I would, of course, notice this!

All of these holidays were very successful and inexpensive. We did our own catering most of the time, and had lots of picnic meals. On one occasion, when it was raining at the time we wanted to picnic, we came to a barn with a roof that projected out from the barn for about 15ft! We were able to draw up under this projecting roof. On another occasion we were motoring alongside Lake Lucerne, looking for a picnic spot at a place where there were almost continuous houses, between the road and the lake. However, when we turned into a narrow road towards the lake, we found a spot with all we needed, including seats!

Chapter 38 — THE MOVE TO HARLOW

I decided to leave Plesseys, and at the age of sixty I was looking for fresh employment! This I soon found with S.T.C. who had started an electromechanical division in Harlow.

But I ought to go back in time, in order to relate some more church experiences. When we moved to Ilford we found a small Baptist fellowship, which was meeting in a hall. It was very lively with some good singing. It had a minister who was a good chairman, and keen on people loving one another! From time to time, folks from the congregation had the opportunity to take part up at the front on the platform.

It was decided to put up a 'proper' church building. Funds came in well, and the building was erected. The liveliness of the hall disappeared, in fact it was now discouraged. The folks with good voices no longer mixed with the congregation — they were formed into a separate group, the choir, who marched in together just before the service was due to start. Now, only the minister did the preaching. It seemed to me, that in becoming more 'reverent' we had become less spiritual and certainly less lively.

Many years previously, when I visited my friend Derwent, he used to play the organ in two separate buildings, one a mere hall, the other a proper church building. Both services were under the same vicar, and he would go from one building to the other. Although it was the same man, the service in the hall was much more lively, than the service in the 'proper' church building! In the New Testament we read of churches in houses! Rom. 16:5; 1 Cor. 16:19 and Col. 4:15. We do not read of anything about the buildings. I have already mentioned that the 'factory fellowship' agreed that their meetings seemed to be 'deeper' and the worship more real than it was in their 'good' churches. They were meeting in a little wooden Scout hut! The Bible says, "— I fear, lest by any means, as the serpent beguiled Eve through his subtilty, so your minds should be corrupted from the simplicity that is in Christ''. 2 Cor. 11:3. I am not here trying to make out any cast iron rule about church buildings, but I am trying to arouse interest, and caution, lest we do stray from simplicity.

I did have a Sunday school class of boys; several gave their hearts to the Lord one week, so on the following Sunday I had planned to talk to them about baptism; but I found that the whole Sunday school was required to go into the church!! and so my plan was frustrated. We are not to act as lords over God's people, but alas we often do. The actual words are, ''Neither as being lords over God's heritage, but being ensamples (examples) to the flock'', 1 Pet. 5:3.

In Harlow, we joined up with an open 'brethren' church. This grew rapidly, and on one occasion when there was a baptismal service, I could not get into the building because there were too many people there!

We were, once again, very fortunate in finding a suitable house. The first house we looked at was good. We told the owner that we had other houses to see. We didn't like the others so much as the first house, and when we went back to the first house, we discovered that, in the meantime, a higher price had been offered by somebody else. The owner had refused to sell it, and had kept it for us, despite the fact we had not given him any idea that we would have it. And he was still asking the original price!

Although I lived close to the factory, I used to stay at work during lunch-times quite often so that I could talk to people about Jesus. At a central factory there was a large dining-room, which catered for the workers in all the three S.T.C. factories. A colleague and I would look for a table where there was seated somebody that we knew, and we would join them in the hope of talking about Jesus. One day we made a special effort in prayer, before going into the dining-room. But we looked in vain for someone to talk to. We agreed that we would both pray again and try again the next day.

During the morning of this next day, a man came to me saying, ''That is a Scripture Union badge that you are wearing, isn't it?'' I said yes and asked him what he knew about the Scripture Union, and whether he was staying to lunch. He said, ''Yes, I don't usually stay, but I am today''. So we were able to have lunch together, and after our chat I invited him and his wife to our house. They came, and we had a good evening, starting with a gramophone record; ''Somebody bigger than you and I'', by Beverly Shea. His wife took down the words in shorthand, and we played the record several times, to enable her to catch all the words. They came again for a second evening, and again for the third evening. It seemed right then to challenge them to accept Christ. This they did, on their knees; on rising the lady said, "I feel all washed inside". They were both baptised in the lively open 'brethren' church, and they continued with us until they moved away from the district.

We had a few conversions and baptisms, but we were not able to build up a fellowship comparable with earlier days. We met strong opposition to baptism, which would have spoiled the needed unity in a fellowship. I think I must have got too much involved in my work, for there should have been more fruit! After a few years, I was moved to the Standard Telephones' Research Laboratories, where I continued to develop relays. Here again, I found that a christian, with whom I would have liked to start building up a fellowship, was a strong opponent of believers' baptism. I had lots of talks with my colleagues, but no conversions.

My work needed me to make a number of visits to Germany and Italy, and finally, in my last year before retirement, to USA, Germany again and Moscow. I had to deliver lectures to national and international conferences on relays in USA and Germany, but in Moscow it was to Russian engineers selected by the government, and mostly to women.

Whilst in USA I was allowed to spend my summer vacation there, and to do part of my journey to the conference centre by road in a car that I hired. I flew to Tulsa and drove to Stillwater, about 80 miles away. I was offered a choice of car and chose a Plymouth. Of course, it had the steering wheel on the left-hand side, it was an automatic gear change, and it had done only 38 miles! So I had to drive this strange new animal right through Tulsa, stopping occasionally to consult my map. All went well, the air-conditioning worked fine and kept the car nice and cool. However, before long the car was getting too cold and I could not see how to switch off the air-conditioning! I think the right switch was labelled 'Dynamo'! I arrived safely at Oklahoma University, in Stillwater, where I stayed in a comfortable hotel which was part of the university. The next morning, I was entertained to breakfast with the folks running the conference. Naturally, I had to be photographed and made a fuss of! They were very warm in their reception — not at all 'stand-offish'.

Before each lecture, somebody would announce the name of the lecturer and then he would leave the platform for the lecturer. I began my lecture by thanking them for my very warm reception, and mentioning that on a previous visit to the States, I went to a baptist church and they asked me to preach on the following Sunday, although I was a stranger to them, and not an official minister. I said this would not happen in England. Then I said, "Now we must get down to business --", the lecture was well received, and I was given a diploma — and made a Fellow in the College of Relay Engineers, an F.C.R.E.

Edith was on holiday with me in the States, staying with our elder daughter Jillian. We started on our journey to the States in the firm's chauffeur-driven car to the airport. VIP treatment! But what about when Jesus comes back? Do you know what the Bible says? "We (born-again ones) shall be caught up --- in the clouds, to meet the Lord in the air: and so shall we ever be with the Lord". 1 Thess. 4:17. Caught up in the clouds to meet the Lord! What about that for VIP treatment? Are you coming with me?

I had only been home a few days, when I had to go off to Germany. This was an international conference, with simultaneous translation into several languages. The audience could listen by headphones to their own choice of language. We lecturers were entertained to a meal and to speeches by the mayor in the Town Hall. We also had a coach trip into Bavaria, which was very pleasant. Beautiful scenery, brilliant sunshine and quite warm despite the snow on the mountains; and, I think, on the roadside too.

About a fortnight later I had to go to Moscow, with several others, to give a paper on relays. The audience was mostly female. Our papers had been translated into Russian, and they were read by various interpreters. The audience was always very attentive and there were a number of questions needing the help of the interpreter.

The Russians entertained us to a very good circus in a permanent building. The proceedings started with us all standing up and singing something which I presume was their National Anthem, but they seemed to take it more seriously than we would take our 'God save the Queen'. On another evening, we were taken to a ballet with about 100 performers on the stage at the same time. Another evening we were taken to a theatre. When the tickets for the theatre were being distributed, some members of our party enquired as to which were the best seats. They were given their tickets for the 'best' seats. When the man distributing the tickets came to me, he said, "Woodhead, I suppose you will take the luck of the draw?" I replied "Yes" and received my ticket.

The tickets had the seat numbers on them, and one was left to find one's own numbered seat. The theatre was divided into large boxes. So I found my seat and sat down, and presently all the heads of our party, including the president of I.T.T. and his wife, came and sat down near me in the same box! and offered me, little me, a chocolate. Lucky Fellow!

H

The play included a scene where nightfall gradually came on, and the stars gradually became visible. It was extremely well done. At the end, there was a big fire at the back of the stage, which also looked very real indeed. The Russians must have put a lot of effort and skill into the performance.

In order to see something of the city, I was about to ask permission to be absent from the lectures for half a day, when the leader came to me with the suggestion that I might like to have some time off. He said go and see the man who arranges our transport, etc. So I saw him, and I was told to go to the enquiry desk of the hotel the next morning at, I think, 9.30 a.m.

There, I found a young lady waiting for me, who could speak perfect English. She took me out of the hotel where, lo and behold! there was a big, black shiny car, and a chauffeur, waiting for us. This took us first to Red Square, and as we were driven along, my young lady guide pointed out all the things of interest. In Red Square, we got out and watched a long file of people paying their respects at Lenin's Tomb. I was a bit surprised that so many people wanted to do this, but I have a suspicion that the Russians do have much more appreciation of their leaders than we realise. Back in the car we would then proceed to some other quarter of interest and alight in order to obtain a better view. We passed through the doctors' quarters and on to the university, where I was told there were a number of American students.

My guide also emphasised that there were a large number of churches functioning in Moscow. But she was surprised when I told her that, back in England, we have many churches that are full, and that many young people go to church. I advised her to go to England and see for herself whenever she had the opportunity, for it is so very easy to have wrong impressions about what goes on in other countries. This tour must have lasted about two hours. It ended with my being set down where the lectures were going on; VIP treatment! Lucky Fellow!

I was due to retire in a few months — my choice, and a bad choice — and it was as though God was arranging for me to go out with a cloud of glory. I was nearly 68 and in excellent health, Lucky Fellow!

The previous year we had had a week's holiday in Dolgellau district of North Wales. We had been very impressed by the beauty of the country surrounding it; and we had seen a bungalow that was waiting for a young man of 68 to put it, and the garden, into shape. We made an offer for it and, as I had feared, the offer was accepted. It became ours and I was wanting to move in. Alas, I had not really waited on the Lord properly. We did pray before making the offer, but I think, now, it was a matter of the Lord letting us

Evening Bible Study

have our own way, more than of Him doing the choosing. But more about that later!

The open brethren church in Harlow grew in numbers rapidly, and it had a large percentage of young people. There was a week-night Bible study held every week. A big proportion of the church went to it so regularly that we knew, whenever there was an absentee, that there was a legitimate reason for it. This Bible study was unusual in that no man, or no one man, ran it! It ran itself — or was it that the Holy Ghost ran it? The elders of the church, that is the official oversight, were rarely present. We had agreed amongst ourselves what portion of the scripture we would study, and we would study it in the order in which it appears in the Bible. It was open for anybody to read or comment as they wished. Since there were several folks with a good knowledge of the Bible, the comments were often quite good and helpful, enabling us to compare scripture with scripture. The Bible says, "Let the word of Christ dwell in you richly in all wisdom; teaching and admonishing one another in psalms and hymns and spiritual songs, singing with grace in your hearts to the Lord". Col. 3:16. Note, it says teaching and admonishing one another. We tend to let one man do the teaching!, so paving the way for such errors as we see in differing churches, because we have done away with the safeguard of other voices. Also, of course, the teaching becomes restricted to what that one man has apprehended; and indeed clearly some churches reveal that restriction in the worship and work.

Chapter 39 — IN DEEPER WATERS

At this point I want to go deeper into the word or God. Some folks will have "lifted their eyebrows" at the suggestion of the teaching being limited in some churches. They may think, "Well, it isn't limited in our church". Be warned, I am now going to drop a bomb! Not every church teaches the way of salvation, as revealed by scripture, which says in one place, "Ye must be born again". In another place it says, "For by grace are ye saved through faith; and that not of yourselves: it is the gift of God: not of works, lest any man should boast". Eph. 2:8, 9. As I have previously written, I attended a number of different churches, over about 17 years, and I did not even know that there was such a thing as conversion.

Why was this essential doctrine not taught? — The answer is quite simple, the teachers had not yet apprehended it, because nobody had taught them! It is likely that sitting in the congregation of some of the churches I attended, there would be some who were converted, but they would not have the opportunity, nor the encouragement to teach others how they got saved. Only the official 'leader' — vicar, minister, priest, pastor — whatever, may do the teaching!; so says custom, convention, tradition. Thus it is easy to see how it came about that the teaching became restricted to one man. It would be because, in total, that one man would have more knowledge and ability than each of the others.

So **Shock No.14:**   There are churches, possibly many, where the way of salvation — the direct command of Christ — is never even taught or permitted to be preached!

So far, I have spoken only of conversion, but there are many other doctrines which get omitted when the teaching is confined to only one person. I have recorded how the doctrine of the second coming of Jesus Christ was omitted in the church I attended. The omission was not due to lack of knowledge, in this case, but in lack

116

of belief. Many teachers have head knowledge of things in the Bible, but which they don't teach because, they just don't believe these particular things. Others may believe them, but they won't normally have the opportunity to teach them, because they have no official position in the church. And there would often be, of course, opposition to the teaching of doctrine which some teachers have not yet apprehended, or had rejected for one reason or another. There are obvious practical difficulties, but take heart, the Bible is a very practical book! It was written under the inspiration of God. 2 Tim. 3:16.

Shock No.15: In some churches Biblical doctrines, which are known and understood, are being restricted or banned from being taught because they are not believed!

We have been looking at many scriptures which are out of harmony with modern thinking and modern practice, and hence it was appropriate for us to prepare our hearts for some shocks. 'God's thoughts are not our thoughts, neither are our ways His ways. For as the heavens are higher than the earth, so are His ways higher than our ways, and His thoughts than our thoughts'. (Isa. 55:8, 9.) "The foolishness of God is wiser than men; and the weakness of God is stronger than men". 1 Cor. 1:25.

There are instances in scripture where God's strategy would appear quite foolish. For example, when it was required to bring down the walls of Jericho, God's strategy was to get Joshua and his army to march round the walls thirteen times, and then shout. Down came the walls! This is written in Josh. 6:1—20. When the children of Israel needed to cross the Red Sea, having neither boats nor aeroplanes, Moses was told, "Lift up thou thy rod, and stretch out thine hand over the sea, and divide it: and the children of Israel shall go on dry ground through the midst of the sea". Exod. 14:16.

We sometimes use the word 'Church' to depict a building or a denomination, but in the Bible it is — the complete body of all believers, who have been 'born again' i.e. twice-born, and have Christ and the Holy Spirit dwelling in them, and they are called 'saints', or 'separated to God ones'. The Church is not a natural company but a supernatural one, because God forms part of it by dwelling in it. If it were a natural company we could devise a system of government using clever, eloquent, well-educated men to rule it, as in the armed forces. But no, it needs God's wisdom to organise it. It is very precious to God, since it cost Him the sacrifice of His only begotten Son, who, contrary to all human expectations, left NO-ONE in charge except Himself. In fact, He left instructions that:— "He that is greatest among you, let him be as the younger: and he that is chief, as he that doth serve", which cuts out any idea

118

of lordship or kingly authority over fellow believers, but a willingness to learn, and to submit to others in meekness.

Very few of us have grasped what the scriptures have said about the need for avoiding 'kingly authority' and 'lordship' in the church. It is common practice, alas, to have a "king" over a local church, although, of course, he does not accept that title — he just rules the church as though he was a king — and his 'subjects', knowing no better expect him to rule the church. They do not expect him to, "be as the younger", or to be a servant. See Luke 22:25, 26.

I am very sure that most of my readers will be amazed at what they have read here. Ponder over it, and reread it, and act upon it, unless you find it unscriptural!

In my own personal experience I have seen much harm by 'bossiness', the exercise of 'kingly' authority. That Bible study group which I have described in the previous chapter, was brought to an end by somebody outside the group exercising 'kingly' authority. Indeed, very many were thereby driven out of the church, and years later that church had not recovered its earlier numbers. Beware of 'bossiness': be clothed with humility.

Having written against there being a 'king' over a local church, it becomes very necessary to dive deeply into the scriptures in order to find out how a church should be run. Of course, one immediately thinks of Jesus Christ who is our perfect example. He was so humble that he washed His disciples' feet. He set up no elaborate organisation. He was prepared to spend time talking to one person, for example the woman at the well; John 4. He rode on a donkey. He refused to act as judge when two people had a quarrel; Luke 12:13, 14. He was willing to go to heal one person; Matt. 8:7. But He was so much a servant that He laid down his own life for us, you and me. Materially, he had not where to lay his head, Matt. 8:20. He had not tribute money, Matt. 17:27.

Yes, materially He was very poor, but spiritually He was very rich. There was no circumstance in which He was not the master. There was no need that He could not meet. He fed 5,000 men with one boy's lunch. He commanded the wind to cease!; He healed the sick; He raised the dead, and He drove out demons. He drove fish into a net. He led, not by being 'bossy', but be being rich spiritually, by being able to do things, and by having a character such that men wanted to follow Him, a character of humility, of love, and of compassion. He had great power because He kept close to His Father.

It is God's purpose that the church should have power. 1 Cor. 4:19, says, "But I will come to you shortly, if the Lord will, and will know, not the speech of them which are puffed up, but the power''. John 14:12 says, "He that believeth on me, the works that I do shall he do also; and greater works than these shall he do; because I go to My Father''.

We will now review what the scriptures have to say about the qualifications of Elders. Are they then to be men of outstanding academic ability, men with university degrees, men of powerful personality, men with leadership qualities? No, once again we shall be brought face to face with God's 'foolishness' which is wiser than men.

We find the qualifications listed in 1 Tim. 3:2—7 and in Titus 1:5—9.

1. Blameless.
2. Husband of one wife.
3. Vigilant.
4. Sober.
5. Of good behaviour.
6. Given to hospitality.
7. Apt to teach.
8. Not given to wine.
9. No striker.
10. Not greedy of filthy lucre.
11. Patient.
12. Not a brawler.
13. Not covetous.
14. One that ruleth well his own house.
15. Not a novice.
16. Having a good report from outsiders.
17. Not self-willed.
18. Not soon angry.
19. A lover of good men.
20. Just.
21. Holy.
22. Temperate.
23. Holding fast the faithful word.

These are discussed in the chapters on Elders and God's rules, (i.e. chpts. 3 & 4) but are reviewed here to emphasise their importance.

Chapter 40 — THE MOVE TO WALES

Let us pause for a while in our pursuit of scriptural truth and go to Wales; the country with much mountain scenery, good roads — and not too much traffic — and grand stretches of sandy beaches. It deserves far more visitors than it gets; although it must be admitted that the sun in summer is less powerful than it is in the South of England.

Our bungalow was built on the side of a mountain, on ground which sloped very steeply down, from the end of the back garden down to the private road. I found that I could climb up the left-hand side of the 'garden' by holding on to the fence, but the right-hand side had huge rocks, and one needed to be a rock climber to get up on that side. No path had been cut to the top of the garden. The vegetation was mainly bracken and gorse bushes, with some surrounding trees. The front gate would be about twenty feet below the bungalow, and about a hundred or more feet above the main road. So there was a grand view from all the front windows, extending all over Fairbourne and Cardigan Bay.

The shops and railway station would be about a quarter of a mile away; and the beach about half a mile away. There is also a minature railway, which runs from the shops down to the beach, and then on to Penryn Point. This railway is very popular with the holiday-makers.

Since I had not yet retired, we hurriedly decorated the bungalow, lightly furnished it, and let it out to holiday-makers, for the first summer. We arrived ourselves at the end of the summer. It proved impossible to get the removal van up our private road, hence it had to be unloaded at the bottom of our road, and the contents brought up in a small lorry. One of the loads included an armchair in the middle of the lorry, and sitting in the chair like a king was one of the removal men!

Fronallt, Wales — 1970

As the removal men had driven through Wales, they were puzzled by signs which kept saying "Llwybr", and pointing in different directions! They said where is that place called "Llwybr"? Llwybr, of course, is not a place at all, it means 'path' or 'footpath'. The Welsh language is not easy, and but few English people seem to be able to master it, in spite of attending classes for that purpose. I personally am hopeless at all languages and particularly so at Welsh! I am guilty of not even making an effort at learning Welsh. During the whole of fourteen years that I have been in Wales, I have not met anybody who could not speak English fluently. Nevertheless, place names and road signs have frequently been changed in recent years to make them more Welsh. Also all official forms now have to be in two languages. It was not like that fourteen years ago.

We found the Welsh people to be very kind and friendly and honest, and hard working, and we have been very happy living amongst them. In business I have never known the language to get in the way, but in our worship it does. I suppose the majority of services in this district are in Welsh. In one small town there is a Welsh Presbyterian Chapel, and an English Presbyterian Chapel, each with but a small congregation and a common minister.

J

Common sense would suggest that they combine, but common sense and sentiment are not good bedfellows. Common sense also would suggest that road signs should not be in two languages, but I suppose I must keep off that subject, because I am a mere engineer!

The conversion of the mountainside into a productive garden was a major project involving thousands of hours of labour. It was necessary of course, to terrace it and to cut a winding path. The ground was a mixture of soil and rocks of various sizes, going up to several tons, and in some places it was just solid rock, sticking out above the general surface. Many of the rocks were too heavy to move and needed to be split up into smaller pieces. The terraces are all built with walls of stones dug out of the ground; what are known as dry-stone walls. Sometimes, when cutting the ground to make the path, the ground before me would be too steep for me to stand upon. I had to cut a few feet in front of me, in order to provide ground flat enough to stand on for cutting the next few feet.

The soil itself is of a very good texture, being the result of some thousands of years of decayed bracken. It has proved excellent for the growing of fruit. Two rows of raspberry canes, each about twenty feet long have produced over forty pounds of fruit each year; and one apple tree, which was about three years old when I planted it, last year has yielded over three hundred pounds of apples. So, there has been some return for all the hard work.

One of my visitors said to me, "I would think you are proud of your garden". But I wasn't, because I was beginning to get a little ashamed of the large amount of time that had gone into it. I was beginning to realize that when I die, I would not be able to take it with me. The Bible says, "lay up for yourselves treasures in heaven, where neither moth nor rust doth corrupt, and where thieves do not break through nor steal: for where your treasure is, there will your heart be also". Matt. 6:20, 21. To some extent, I was repeating the error I made whilst I was farming: the error of putting God into second place. I am a very slow learner, but I am still trying to learn not to lay up for myself, my treasures upon earth. (Matt. 6:19).

There is a Welsh Presbyterian Chapel close by where they used to have services in English from time to time. But those occasions became less frequent and so it became obvious that there was a need to start regular services in English. In conjunction with two mature christians we did start regular services, making use of the chapel building when it was available. Our services followed just after the Welsh services on a Sunday morning.

We were quite free from denominational authority, quite free to follow the Bible as we understood it. There were nineteen of us on the first Sunday and a few more the next Sunday. We had five baptisms, in the sea, one year. We met opposition from a high church vicar, which took away from us one family, just as they were getting interested in baptism. Even after a number of years, we still did not have a Sunday school for the children. Edith and I had left it for younger people to become teachers. But we had made a mistake, we should have taught them ourselves, until such time as the younger ones became willing to take on the task. I suppose we both wanted to rest on Sunday afternoons!

Some of our older members died, and the time came when we thought it would be better for us, and for the holiday-makers, if we all went to a Baptist church just a few miles away. This we did, and last year the numbers attending, in the summer, became so great that we had to hold our services in a secondary school hall, where the accommodation was much bigger.

The author and his wonderful wife, Edith — 1971 (Lucky Fellow!)

Chapter 41 — HEALING THE SICK? — TODAY?

When we were still holding services in the nearby chapel I mentioned in the last chapter, and before we moved to the Baptist church further away, one Sunday morning there came a man, weak on his legs, who needed someone to help him walk. I was standing just outside the chapel door when this man and his helping companion arrived. A very strange thing happened. God filled me with compassion for this man, so weak on his legs. No, don't misunderstand me, it was not ordinary compassion, it was supernatural compassion. The thought went through my mind, that we in the chapel can minister to his spiritual needs, but we can not do anything about his legs. And, of course, it was also brought home to me that it was not like that in the early days of the church. You remember Peter outside the gate Beautiful, saying to the cripple, who was lame from his mother's womb, "In the name of Jesus Christ of Nazareth, rise up and walk". I felt strongly that our ministry should also include healing of the body, and I made up my mind that I would do something about it, next time I was taking the service. So, on the following Sunday, I invited anybody wishing for prayer for healing to come to the front, feeling fairly sure that nobody would respond to the invitation. But I was wrong, one woman came out immediately. We prayed for her and I did hear later that she did derive physical benefit. That was the beginning of my doing anything about ministering physical healing.

Perhaps I ought here to record another occasion, some years later I think. I was taking the service in the Baptist chapel when I said, "We have a fine, healthy-looking crowd of young people here today. Hands up all those who have nothing physically wrong with them whatsoever". As expected, a lot of hands went up. Then I said, "Hands up all those who do have something wrong with them physically". A lot of hands went up. "Now, hands up all those who would like prayer for their physical defects''. A smaller number of hands went up, indicating that there were those who did not wish for prayer!

Now I said, "We are going to forget about our own defects and we are each going to pray for another. Will all those who did raise their hands please step out into the aisles and form themselves into pairs, so that each one of a pair can pray for the other. But I am going to pray first. Let each of you place his right hand on the left shoulder of your partner. Lord, you said in Mark 16:18, 'They shall lay hands on the sick, and they shall recover', please do it''. I did enjoy that prayer! Some of our own folks told me afterwards of benefit from the prayers, but, as many of the folks were holiday-makers, I could not tell the full amount of benefit. But I do like to quote the word of God — to God!

Imagine a little boy going on holiday, and his father promising him that he will buy him a boat to float in the sea. After they have arrived, the boy says, "Daddy, you promised to buy me a boat!" What can daddy do? he has to keep his promise and buy the lad his boat. Is it any different with God? No! God not only has to, but wants to keep His promises. Yes, I really enjoyed asking God to heal all those folks who were having hands laid on them! — because God had made a promise.

K

Chapter 42 — EDITH'S GREAT PROMOTION

My dear wife, Edith, had a stroke, or rather a succession of three strokes, each making her weaker than before. It became necessary for me to become nurse-housekeeper. I read in the Bible some scriptures, which I thought were very helpful and I learnt them off by heart. One was, "Cast thy burden upon the Lord, and he shall sustain thee: he shall never suffer the righteous to be moved". Ps. 55:22. After the third stroke, Edith had several months in hospital before she died.

A few hours before, I had a call from the hospital and I knew what to expect. As I motored along to the hospital, I quoted this scripture to God, "Lord, you have said in your word, 'Fear thou not; for I am with thee: be not dismayed; for I am thy God: I will strengthen thee; yea, I will help thee; yea, I will uphold thee with the right hand of my righteousness'. (Isa. 41:10.) Please do it!" and did He? Yes, He certainly did. He gave me strength to fix up all the details. The notice to go in the paper, with the dates of the burial and of a memorial service in the chapel, etc., etc. It seemed that everybody whom I needed to contact was there ready to be contacted! I arranged that a close christian friend would speak at the graveside, and that close christian friends would handle the coffin. The singing at the graveside was grand, and God even gave me strength to refer to Revn. 19:7, where it says, "Let us be glad and rejoice, and give honour to him: for the mariage of the Lamb is come, and his wife hath made herself ready".

The day after Edith's home call, I was due to take the service in the chapel. My daughter, Jillian, said to me, "You can't take the service, Daddy!" I said, "I can". And I had no difficulty until I was praying, and then I choked up because God had been so good to me, in giving me such a wonderful wife, and for letting me have her for over fifty years! I was so full of gratitude to God for what he had done for me, and also for the great promotion of Edith to be with dear Lord Jesus.

A few days later, at the memorial service in the evening, we sang "Turn your eyes upon Jesus, Look full in His wonderful face, And the things of earth will grow strangely dim, In the light of His glory and grace". Our close friend, Pam Worsey sang a solo, "The stranger of Galilee". I quoted from Prov. 1:5, "A wise man will hear, and will increase learning; and a man of understanding shall attain unto wise counsels". I gave my testimony, starting with Edith requiring me to become a full member of the church, and ending with her conversion, and her singing, "Jesus gave her water that was not in the well". Then we all sang that chorus, and I quoted, as strongly as I possibly could the words in Matt. 18:3, "Verily I say unto you, Except ye be converted, and become as little children, ye shall not enter into the kingdom of heaven".

Our friend, Mr Ben Baker gave a word from Revn. 14:13, "Blessed are the dead which die in the Lord from henceforth: Yea, saith the Spirit, that they may rest from their labours; and their works do follow them".

We all sang:—

"Like a river glorious
Is God's perfect peace,
Over all victorious,
In its bright increase;
Perfect, yet it floweth
Fuller every day;
Perfect, yet it groweth,
Deeper all the way".

One of our friends commented favourably on the service afterwards, but remarked that, 'he did not agree with us'! Since we had gone to great lengths to be absolutely scriptural, I am forced to the sad conclusion that really he was disagreeing with the word of God. He was religious and in fact, an Anglican organist. Dear reader, please take note of the word of God and don't let anything else take its place. In our Lord's time, only a few of the religious people accepted him, the majority were opposed to him, and some engineered his cruel crucifixion. When Billy Graham was here last year, none of the vicars or ministers in this area of Wales supported him! Why not? You must be the judge; one day they will have to face the author of the Bible! and explain why they did not support Billy Graham, who is obviously such an ardent supporter of the Bible.

"Except ye be converted -- ye shall not enter into the kingdom of heaven''. It is not sufficient to have a head belief, that Jesus died to atone for the sins of the world. I had that belief, but I was not converted. It is not sufficient to have a head knowledge, that Jesus died for you, in your place. I had that knowledge, but I was not converted. It is not sufficient to become religious and to attend some church or chapel. I did that, but I was not converted.

No, there is really only one way to be converted, and that is to receive Jesus into our hearts, confessing and repenting of our sins, if and when we are made aware of them. The scripture says, ''He that hath the Son hath life; and he that hath not the Son of God hath not life''. 1 John 5:12. ''He that believeth not the Son shall not see life; but the wrath of God abideth on him''. John 3:36.

You may not believe that there is the devil, satan, but that won't remove him. He is the god of this world. ''The god of this world hath blinded the minds of them which believe not, lest the light of the glorious gospel of Christ, who is the image of God, should shine unto them''. 2 Cor. 4:4.

(It is worth mentioning here that some of the events of the next chapter occurred before Edith went home to be with the Lord, and some were experienced by Stanley, together with friends or members of his family, after she had been 'promoted'.   *A.B.*)

Chapter 43 — VISIT TO AMERICA

Both of our daughters married Americans, and then settled down in America. Our first grandchild was about nine months old when we made our first visit, and naturally we were wanting to see him! Jillian and her husband Robert were then living on the outskirts of an industrial town known as Alton, in Illinois. Population, about 100,000. We were taken to a 'drive-in' cafe, where, without getting out of the car, we spoke our order into a microphone, and it was delivered onto a shelf close to the car window.

A new shopping area had been built just outside the town. It consisted of a large rectangular car park adjoining the main road, with shops around the remaining three sides. It seemed so simple and convenient, and so free from congestion. In the main road of Alton, Edith and I stood and watched the traffic and the people crossing the road and we came to the conclusion that, contrary to our expectation, the speeds were lower than in England. We had thought that the Americans were always in a hurry, but it is just not true. At crossroads near a school, the traffic was controlled by the children themselves, without any adult being present. They had flags on poles, and when they lowered the poles to the horizontal position, the traffic stopped to allow the children to cross the road to go to school.

We visited Niagara Falls, and went into one of the power stations where a film was already being shown to the visitors. When the lights were turned up at the end of the film, we were surprised at the large number of school children present, because there had not been any noise. Edith complimented one of the teachers on the excellent behaviour of the children, and she was told that, "We have learnt our lesson, we used to have free discipline, but now we don't".

Our journey to Niagara was by plane, from Chicago to Buffalo.

129

It was near to midnight, when we arrived at Buffalo, and Edith wondered if we would be able to find a room in a hotel at that late hour! But my short experience of America, was that one seems to be able to get what one wants at abnormal hours! We were very soon fixed up OK in a comfortable hotel, and when we returned, a few minutes later, to the airport, we had no difficulty in getting something to eat at midnight. A black lady offered to make us toast!

When viewing Niagara, I was amazed at the huge volume of water flowing over the falls, and at the amount of power generated at the power stations — over a million kilowatts.

Near to Chicago we had lunch with a Jewish family; my son-in-law's brother and his wife. They asked us, "What does Billy Graham preach?" As we began to tell them, they became so interested that they sent their children out of the room so that they would not be interrupted and Edith and I were talking on that subject until it was nearly tea-time, some hours later! In England one does not meet, generally, such readiness to listen to what Billy Graham preaches.

In Chicago Billy Graham was preaching in a large auditorium which held, I think 40,000 people. We timed our visit to Chicago to coincide with Billy's campaign, in the hope that we would be able to persuade Robert's Jewish mother, and her catholic companion, to come and hear Billy. We discovered, however, that they had already arranged to take us and had reserved seats for us all!

Some years later I was staying with them in Chicago, when they took me to the Moody Memorial Chapel. The service on that particular Sunday was designed especially for visitors, and the sermon was a very clear exposition on the way of salvation. God certainly knew how to arrange things! The catholic companion had arthritis badly, and she asked me to pray for her healing. This I did, and she has testified to receiving great benefit from the prayer, that has lasted for years. She described me as an angel sent from heaven! I am no angel, but I have a God who keeps his word. Am I not a 'Lucky Fellow'?

I would like to pass on to you a few more incidents. While I was staying in St. Louis with my daughter Jillian and her family, she had driven into a garage to buy petrol, and her way out required her to cross the road and get into the far stream of traffic. The adjacent stream was stationary, because the traffic lights were red. When the stream started to move Jillian said to me, "Daddy, there's no way I'll get through that line of traffic". I replied, "Oh, I don't know about that!" and I prayed silently to my dear heavenly Father, "Father, you have somebody very precious in this car; somebody

The Prayer Tower — 1983

for whom your dear Son gave his life, please make a way for us". Immediately, the lorry driver opposite to us pulled up and signalled for us to get in front of him into the line of traffic, a very unusual event in America! Am I a 'Lucky Fellow'? No, just one of God's VIPs. A few days later, Jillian was taking me to the airport. She was late starting off, and then discovered that she would need to buy petrol, so that there was really no hope of arriving at the airport in time for the plane. She said to me, "Daddy, you had better pray". But this time I didn't pray, for I felt dear Lord Jesus had the matter under control. It did seem a bit unfair that Jillian had all the worry, whilst I sat beside her without a care in the world! At the airport, we stopped at an unauthorised place, and we arrived at the departure gate five minutes after the plane was supposed to have departed. But the flight had been held up and the plane was five minutes late! and I got on it! Again 'Lucky Fellow'? No, just one of God's VIPs.

During another visit to Jillian, she asked me, "Was there anything you particularly wanted to see in America?" I replied that I would like to see the Oral Roberts building in Tulsa. She said,

"I'll take you". But when I discovered it was 400 miles away, I refused her offer. However, she was very persistent, and I really wanted to have her to myself for a while, so I let her take me. Although we did not leave St. Louis before 10 a.m. we were in Tulsa by early evening, in spite of the fact that we did not travel at more than 60 miles per hour.

We found that the hotel was just on the opposite side of the road to the Oral Roberts set-up, and that my bedroom had an uninterrupted view of all the lovely buildings — 'Lucky Fellow'. After we had eaten we went across the road to a building that was lit up, and we learned that a seminar was due to start in a few minutes. We were allowed to join in, and we were given lots of needful items, meal tickets, note pad, etc. and told that there would be a Bible on each seat. We were not asked for any money! So without having any prior knowledge we had arrived just in time to join a seminar, that we did not know was on! "Lucky Fellow(s)" — again!

I think that there were about 4,000 in the audience. The Roberts family were up on the platform, and we greatly enjoyed the straightforward, simple ministry, and the loving atmosphere. The next day we were there all day; seminars in the morning and evening, and viewing of many other of the buildings, during the afternoon; including the City of Faith, which is a clinic of 60 floors, a hospital and a medical research center: all very high quality, beautiful buildings.

The next day, Saturday, we were due to motor 400 miles home: nevertheless Jillian decided that she wanted to attend the Saturday a.m. seminar! We left Tulsa a little after midday, and were home by the middle of the evening. Jillian and I had a little prayer of thanksgiving to God, for having arranged it all so wonderfully. What 'Lucky Fellows'!

On a previous visit, Jillian needed to go to a beautiful island, known as Hilton Head Island, South Carolina, where her husband owned a Holiday House. The journey was about 800 miles each way. We travelled in a large Buick car, taking with us Jillian's friend Nancy, who took turns with the driving. On the way the car 'played up', it would not go at more than 35 miles per hour up a slight slope. It was Nancy's turn at the wheel, and she remarked, "In no way will this car go up Great Smoky Mountains in this condition". We had planned to go over Great Smoky Mountains where the road ascends to 6,000ft in one place. We stopped at a garage for inspection, but the mechanic could not find the fault. It was time to put up for the night. Jillian said to me, "I don't know how we shall manage tomorrow, Daddy". I replied, "We shall be alright''. It was inconceivable to me that it could be otherwise.

Shortly after we set off the next day, I had a word with the Lord. "Lord, you are a wonderful engineer; you made human beings with all of their marvellous bits and pieces. This car is a very simple contraption by comparison; please mend it''. I was praying silently, of course, and directly I had finished, Nancy, who was driving again, said, "I can't find anything wrong with this car this morning''. We were only on the flat. I told her about my prayer and how her remark coincided with the ending of my prayer. When we came to the Great Smoky Mountains, the car went 'like a dream'. I had never before enjoyed such 'effortless' power. The car had 8 cylinders — and lots of cc's.

The island has lots of trees, and when one motors down the main shopping street, one has to peer between the trees in order to see any shops! There is a lovely beach of white firm sand, and as one comes off the beach, there are provided water hoses for washing off the sand. There is a golf course, with ponds containing alligators! The temperature was just over 100° F in the shade. I had to keep out of the sun!

My younger daughter Dawn, and her family, live in Shaker Heights, near to Cleveland beside Lake Erie. I suppose Shaker Heights is really a very large residential suburb of Cleveland. It has very many large houses situated on the tree-lined roads, and is very pleasant. We used to go to what is called 'The Chapel' for worship. This was very well attended, and everything was very well done. It was under the oversight of a number of elders. It had a choir which came onto the platform to sing, and then returned to sit with the congregation. Nobody wore clerical garb. It had a simplicity which I found scriptural. "I fear, lest by any means, as the serpent beguiled Eve through his subtilty, so your minds should be corrupted from the simplicity that is in Christ''. 2 Cor. 11:3.

One morning, when my stay with Dawn and her family was nearing an end, I prayed that the whole family would go together, to a place of worship, on this my last Sunday. I made the suggestion to the family and heard that a neighbour had arranged to take the two boys to some game or other! I prayed silently to God, saying, "This will be hard for you to fix, Lord!'' But the Lord fixed it, and we were all together in 'The Chapel'. Praise Him!

In both St. Louis and Shaker Heights I spent much time watching christian broadcasts on TV. Almost all day long there are sound Bible-based broadcasts on certain channels. The response from listeners who phone in for prayer is so great that no less than 60 phones have to be manned to deal with them! The broadcasts go

134

Workshop — 1990

out to forty countries, including Lebanon and Italy, but not to Great Britain! I am speaking of 1983. I was amazed at both the quality and the quantity of these Bible-based broadcasts. In Great Britain there seems to have been a slight improvement in the broadcasting of Bible truths, in recent times, but we have a very long way to go yet, before the Bible has its rightful place in our broadcasts.

---------- We need 'born-again' directors of broadcasting! ----------

On one of the earlier trips I had Edith with me. She was then able to walk just a little, so I had to help her, and manage the luggage. It was not easy but we managed. At the Gatwick airport we were driven on a little electric buggy down to the plane: we felt like VIPs. At other airports we had the aid of wheelchairs, and several times we were allowed to board the plane before the other passengers. On the way home I had requested a wheelchair at the airport, and since this had not arrived as soon as I expected, I had to remind the attendant at the desk of that fact. Presently all the passengers for our flight moved forward out of the lounge, and still no wheelchair! I had to go to the desk again to 'ginger them up'. They assured me that they would not leave me behind, and they went in search of the wheelchair. At last it arrived and we proceeded out of the lounge — into another lounge beside the departure gate. There were all the other passengers still waiting, and we had not been left behind! Furthermore, the wheelchair was pushed right up to the departure gate and we were the first on the plane. The attendant said, "You were quite worried, were you not?" and I had to admit that I was. So you see, my faith in my Lord was very lacking then — perhaps it had not developed so much then as it did later.

Dear reader, I want to say to you, don't be like me! I am a very late developer for I am 86, and I have been a Christian for about 54 years, and it is really only in the last few years that my faith has blossomed out into healing of the sick — and that not very much yet. You might think that a man of 86 has 'had it'! But I am expecting greater things yet. "Those that be planted in the house of the Lord shall flourish in the courts of our God. They shall still bring forth fruit in old age; they shall be fat and flourishing; To shew that the Lord is upright: He is my rock, and there is no unrighteousness in Him". Psalm 92:13—15.

Chapter 44 — CONCLUSION TO PART 3

No-one can write their own complete autobiography! and I feel sorry that this cannot be complete, for I am expecting many more miracles yet!

It falls to me now to pass on some parting thoughts. The earlier chapters on church organisation, (Part 1:— Today's Church --God's Design), contain much that is out of line with most modern practice and modern thinking. It will take a lot of humility and courage to put the Bible, the word of God, where it should be. It will take a lot of swimming against the tide. Many have lost their lives by confronting religious people with the error of their ways! Jesus lost his life that way. But Jesus said, "---- he that loseth his life for my sake shall find it". Matt. 10:39(b). "The fear of man bringeth a snare: but whoso putteth his trust in the Lord shall be safe". Prov. 29:25.

I would like to mention some of the books that have helped me:—

Miracle Valley.	Jim Wilkinson.
I Believe in Miracles.	Kathryn Kuhlman.
Gentle Breezes.	Mel Tari.
Ever Increasing Faith.	Smith Wigglesworth.
Victory Miracle Library.	Morris Cerullo.
Various publications, by:—	Oral Roberts.

These all contain records of miracles, and are hardly likely to appeal to those whose minds are set against miracles! But nevertheless, they in particular need to read them! In Acts 9:34, 35, we read that Peter said to Aeneas, "Jesus Christ maketh thee whole: arise, and make thy bed. And he arose immediately". Aeneas had been in bed eight years with the palsy. In the next verse (v.35) we read, 'all that dwelt at Lydda and Saron saw him, and turned to the Lord'. Just one miracle of healing — and two whole towns turned to the Lord!

God said, "So shall my word be that goeth forth out of my mouth: it shall not return unto me void, but it shall accomplish that which I please, and it shall prosper in the thing whereunto I sent it. For ye shall go out with joy, and be led forth with peace: the mountains and the hills shall break forth before you into singing, and all the trees of the field shall clap their hands". Isaiah 55:11, 12.

Much love to you, dear reader, be 'spiritually fat and flourishing', Psalm 92:14(b).

Your aged brother in Christ,
Stanley Woodhead — "Lucky fellow!" (p.92.)

138

Appendix — SUMMARY OF SHOCKS!

No. 1: Jesus did not appoint anyone to take his place after He left.

No. 2: The most able apostles were to be learners, submitting to others and serving them.

No. 3: Churches must have elders ordained in them.

No. 4: Elders have prime responsibility! Not to assist the pastor (etc.) but OVER everybody and to ensure the church is fed.

No. 5: It is wrong to appoint ONE man to do all the ministry, and worse to expect him to take the oversight as well.

No. 6: Overseers do not need a college education nor university degree! A man straight from college would be a novice, and may have no family wherein to prove his ruling ability.

No. 7: God chooses a man lacking in basic leadership qualities for a difficult leadership role!

No. 8: There is no direct mention of human christian church LEADERS in the New Testament.

No. 9: Church members (the sheep), should teach and admonish one another!

No.10: The Kingdom of God is not in word, but in Power!

No.11: To be true to scripture, the title Reverend can apply only to God and not to any man, — not even great men like Paul.

No.12: God still chooses speakers, quite unsuitable by human standards, and then performs miracles to enable them to do the impossible!

No.13: God gives a totally non-musical person the ability to sing with such joy he shed tears, and experiences the joy of the Lord.

No.14: There are churches where the direct command of Christ, teaching the way of salvation, is neither taught nor permitted to be.

No.15: Although known and understood, certain Bible doctrines are being restricted or not allowed to be taught, because they are not believed!

"Whatsoever things are true, whatsoever things are honest -----think on these things", from Philippians 4:8.

*Be Ye Doers of the Word,
and not Hearers only, --*

Jas. 1:22.